Under-standing Spiritual Warfare

Published by SONLIFE INTERNATIONAL

Distributed by
NEW LEAF PRESS
HARRISON, ARKANSAS 72601 USA

UNDERSTANDING SPIRITUAL WARFARE
© Copyright 1984 by
Roger V. Houtsma
All Rights Reserved
ISBN 089-221-125-3
Distributed by New Leaf Press, Harrison, Ark.
Printed in the United States of America

Dedication

I am dedicating this book to my loving wife, Janice, who has stood faithfully with me in many battles through which the truths in this book have been lived out.

CONTENTS

UNDERSTANDING SPIRITUAL WARFARE

Introduction

Jesus said, "Ye shall know the truth and the truth shall make you free." John 8:32

There are many individuals who are frightened and disturbed about studying the domain of darkness. Many are in bondage because it is the enemy's desire that they stay ignorant. Paul writes, "We are not ignorant of his [Satan's] devices" (2 Cor, 2:11). You cannot fight an enemy you do not understand, and succeed. You cannot fight a sophisticated battle and gain the victory if you do not know what is happening and if you do not know how the enemy functions.

There is much to be covered in order to understand this subject, and there is much that will have to be left unsaid. We will look at Satan, his origin and fall, what demons and fallen angels are, something about their kingdom, God's solution, and what warfare is all about. You cannot hit the target until you locate it; if you do not locate the enemy, you are not going to overcome him. As Christians, our posture is not as one holding the fort, for we must be aggressive. The Kingdom of Heaven suffers aggression and the aggressive take it by force (Matt. 11:12), and we need to be aggressive against the kingdom of darkness. We are in a war whether we like it or not; we are in a war whether we understand it or not; and those who do not understand it often become tremendous tools of the enemy, even though they think they are serving God. Lies and ignorance will bind; truth sets free. If you believe something to be true that is in fact a lie, that lie will operate in your life just as if it were truth.

For example, if you heard a big bang, followed by someone coming in and telling you that your car had just been blown up by a stick of dynamite, and if you believed it, you would have a certain reaction and respond accordingly whether the testimony that was brought to you was true or not.

That is how a lie works, as if it were truth. When the enemy deceives us and causes us to believe something to be true that is in

viii

fact a lie, we are in bondage to it. If the enemy tells you that it is God's will for you to be afflicted with sickness and disease, and you believe it, then your response to the Lord is going to be very different than if you believed it was God's will to heal you and make you whole. If you believed there was no answer for your marriage problem, your response would be much different than if you understood that God wanted to make your marriage work and that He was able to do so.

Truth sets free, lies bring into bondage, and the devil's great purpose is to keep the world ignorant of himself and of his ways. He wants to confuse the issue; he wants us to blame him for what we do, and he wants us to blame ourselves for what he does.

Today, we are living in an hour when there is a special onslaught of deceiving spirits in the church and in the world. In the mid-fifties we found a church in America that had lost its power and was on the decline. We found that people were falling away from Christianity in this country right and left. This produced a generation with an American model of life which did not have God in it. The result was a generation which was hungry for spiritual experience. Looking for those spiritual experiences, they could not find them in dead churches so they looked elsewhere: drugs, education, pleasure, activity, position. In response many people who knew God recognized they had fallen from Him and began to seek the Lord for their children and families and friends and God began to bring a harvest to America. There began to be a revival, known as the Charismatic Renewal.

In the wake of this generation of searching young people came a worldwide change: a change in lifestyle, a change in mentality or social consciousness, a change in orientation to the world, which reflected values borne out of the kingdom of darkness and the drug culture. In its wake came all kinds of occultism and spiritism, new religions and all kinds of means through which people would seek for answers.

That should not seem strange to us because it is a fulfillment of prophecy about the last days. One of the signs for the last days would be a tremendous revival of deceiving spirits of the enemy (Matt. 24:4-5, 11). As a result, all believers should welcome knowledge that will enable them to pass through this time in church history without being ensnared by the enemy's wiles or traps, in order to be able to live free and in victory and to help those who have been trapped by the enemy.

IT IS POSSIBLE, EVEN AS A CHRISTIAN WHO LOVES GOD AND WANTS HIM WITH ALL THEIR HEART, IN IGNORANCE TO STAND AGAINST WHAT GOD IS DOING AND DEFEND WHAT THE DEVIL IS DOING. Lack of understanding will cause you to take positions that are incorrect.

Many people do not want to rock the boat. They have been influenced in their thinking by the values of secular humanism and situation ethics. If you *really* share Christ, it's going to rock the boat; it will knock someone out of neutral. If they don't respond positively, they will try to run from it. They may take offense and be negative if they haven't received. What often follows is a humanistic thought passing through your mind that says, "You are awfully intolerant of someone else's religion. Who are you to run around and try to press what you believe on someone else? Aren't *you* a bigot?" YOU HAVE AN OBLIGA-TION AS THE ONE WHO KNOWS THE TRUTH. YOU ARE TO PROCLAIM IT REGARDLESS OF THE RE-SPONSE OF THE PEOPLE WHO HEAR IT, BECAUSE THEIR ETERNAL DESTINY LIES IN THE HANDS OF THE TRUTH THAT YOU HAVE IN YOUR HEART. *If you don't proclaim the message, you have failed them. That means you will have to go against the demonic doctrine in our culture which tells you that you should be tolerant, that you should not be trying to press your religion on anyone.*

I do not mean that you shouldn't have wisdom in your witness, but you should be aware of what is going on. The Scripture says that the god of this world, Satan, has blinded the hearts and minds of those who believe not lest the light of the gospel would shine into their heart and they should be converted (2 Cor. 4:4). That means that every time you witness, you are meeting a demonic resistance which is trying to blind the heart and mind of that individual from the truth. Often, when you find a reaction to your witness, there is demonic activity from the kingdom of darkness behind it. *To bow down to any doctrine that says you shouldn't ruffle feathers is to bow down to devilish lies that want*

*to keep you ignorant of the fact that you are in a spiritual warfare,
and allow the enemy to continue to have free sway in this world
because of your ignorance!*

Whosoever therefore shall confess me before men, him will
I confess also before my Father which is in heaven. But
whosoever shall deny me before men, him will I also deny
before my Father which is in heaven. Think not that I am
come to send peace on earth: I came not to send peace, but a
sword. For I am come to set a man at variance against his
father, and the daughter against her mother, and the
daughter in law against her mother in law. And a man's foes
shall be they of his own household. He that loveth father or
mother more than me is not worthy of me: and he that loveth
son or daughter more than me is not worthy of me. And he
that taketh not his cross, and followeth after me, is not
worthy of me. He that findeth his life shall lose it: and he that
loseth his life for my sake shall find it. Matt. 10:32-39

We come to know truth through God's Word. We need to
study the Word and to know what it says. When you know truth,
it keeps you out of deception. That Word must also be worked
into your experience. As you get truth worked out in your life
experientially, the truth of the written Word is fulfilled in you.

When it comes to a battle in the Spirit, your experience is not
what is going to help you stand. You might have been slain in the
Spirit one hundred times, prayed for forty people who were
instantly healed of cancer, had fifty three-dimensional
technicolor visions, been called out of your body and walked
around heaven, but when you come into warfare the thing that is
going to help you is not going to be any of those experiences—IT
IS GOING TO BE THE WORD OF GOD LAID IN YOUR
HEART.

We find an increase of knowledge in this generation. Daniel
said that in the end-time, knowledge shall be increased. In three to
five years every major field of education is outdated because the
increase of knowledge has been so vast. People getting saved
today are coming out of all kinds of false concepts. They will not
simply be loved out of deception. You can put your arms around

them and say, "I love you and Jesus loves you," pat them on the back, take them out to dinner, buy them a new suit, do everything you can do, but that will not release them from deception. When a person is in deception, the only way they get free is to be taught, line upon line, precept upon precept, and the *truth* will set them free. Nothing else will do it. They will be transformed by the renewing of their mind, the power of truth. We do need to love, but that is not enough. We are to MINISTER THE TRUTH IN LOVE.

1

Dealing With Deception

In the Garden of Eden we see a picture of the first deceptive efforts of Satan with God's creation of man. Man was not full in knowledge when he was placed in the garden. He was innocent; he did not know good and he did not know evil. In order to know evil, he would have to experience it. God had given a commandment that they were not to eat of the Tree of the Knowledge of Good and Evil. Most of us realize this does not refer to an apple tree. There was something more that was meant here, something real. I believe that "something real" was more than a tree and had more depth of meaning and relationship than an apple tree, for certainly knowledge is as tangible as a tree.

It says in Genesis 3:1 that "The serpent was more subtle than any beast of the field which the Lord had made. And he said unto the woman, Yea, hath God said, Ye shall not eat of every tree of the garden?" He questioned God first of all.

"And the woman said unto the serpent, We may eat of the fruit of the trees of the garden: But of the fruit of the tree which is in the midst of the garden, God hath said, Ye shall not eat of it, neither shall ye touch it, lest ye die" (vv 2, 3)" Because of this question coming to her mind, two things happened: She added this statement, "You shall not touch it." God did not say they couldn't touch it. And then she said, *"lest* ye die" when God said, "You shall *surely* die." That is a direct contradiction of what God said.

"For God doth know that in the day ye eat thereof, then your eyes shall be opened, and ye shall be as gods" (v 5). You will be godlike and you will know good and evil.

"When the woman saw that the tree was good for food, and that it was pleasant to the eyes, and a tree to be desired to make one wise, she took of the fruit thereof, and did eat, and gave also unto her husband with her; and he did eat. And the eyes of them both were opened, and they knew that they were naked; and they sewed fig leaves together" (vv 6, 7).

Eve was beguiled by the enemy. She believed a lie. Satan's first work as deceiver is portrayed here under the guise of seeking to lead a human being closer to God, but bringing them into bondage to himself. The bait: "You will be wise like God. You are going to be like God—godlike." First Timothy 2:14 tells us that Eve was deceived.

Deception means you sincerely believe something to be true that is not true. Sincerity is not enough when it comes to the truth.

Eve was perfectly sincere. Adam was not deceived. He *knew* that it was against God's will to partake, but he decided to go along with his wife against God's command. When God encountered them with their sin, Adam said, "It isn't my fault, it's that woman you gave me." And Eve said, "It wasn't my fault, it was that serpent you put in the garden." The next step logically in that progression is, "Well, God, actually it's your fault because you put the serpent there." This illustrates an important principle: EVERY JUSTIFICATION AND RATIONALIZATION THAT YOU MAKE FOR SIN YOU YOUR LIFE IS AN ACCUSATION AGAINST GOD!

When Eve was deceived, notice that Satan said, "You will be like God." He didn't say, "Go and eat of the Tree of the Knowledge of Good and Evil and you will be like demons." He didn't want to tell the truth because if he did, they wouldn't want it. So he misrepresented it, and deceived them because they "bought into the lie." We find his objective was to get Eve to disobey God. "Disobey God to be like God."

God came and dealt with Satan:

> The Lord God said unto the serpent, Because thou hast done this, thou art cursed above all cattle, and above every beast of the field; upon thy belly shalt thou go, and dust shalt thou eat all the days of thy life. And I will put enmity between thee and the woman, and between thy seed and her seed; it shall bruise thy head, and thou shalt bruise his heel. Gen. 3:14-15

Satan triumphed in this encounter with man. He deceived man and brought him into sin, breaking relationship with God, and with devastating consequences. Notice that with all of his sweet talk, *his motivation and purpose was destruction.* Don't ever compromise with an enemy who is out to destroy you. Don't ever have any good thoughts toward him. The enemy has no good in him; he will not repent, he will never be redeemed, he will be eternally damned according to the Word (Rev. 20:10). Don't give him any space. Every chance you get to give him a good lick, give him three.

"And I will put enmity between thee and the woman, and between thy seed an her seed; it shall bruise thy head, and thou shalt bruise his heel." Satan triumphed in the encounter, but GOD OVERRULED. The victim, who was the woman, would become the vehicle for the advent of the victor, the incarnation of the Christ. When the seed of the woman came, He was going to destroy the works of the devil (1 John 3:8). Since this announcement in God's Word, the history of man has been the story of a war between these two seeds: the seed of the serpent and the seed of the woman.

If we were to do a quick Bible study, we would see what happened. Adam and Eve had children, Cain and Abel. Abel offered an offering that was acceptable to God and He put His hand of blessing on Abel, while Satan was wondering which one would be the progenitor of the seed that would destroy him. Cain was disobedient and did not want to follow God's way of sacrifice, so Satan worked in Cain until he killed Abel, because there was enmity between the seed of the serpent and the seed of the woman. In the first generation we see murder, inspired by the devil.

Seth was born and became the next progenitor. We find that the Scripture says *nephilim* (the Hebrew word for "giants") were in the earth (Gen. 6). Apparently, angelic beings who left their first estate and cohabited with man (either spiritually or physically) brought perversion into the human race and these "giants" were the result. The entire human race became so perverted and twisted that God came to Noah and said that He was going to destroy the earth, preserve Noah, and start over again. Noah and his family were preserved in the ark and there was destruction on the earth. As soon as that happened, one of Noah's sons saw him in his nakedness and because of his sinful response a curse came upon him.

After a period of time Abraham was called and had a son, Isaac, the promised child and progenitor. Before Isaac, Abraham had another son, Ishmael, and Satan got Ishmael upset with Isaac and began to bring hatred and enmity between them.

Later, we find that Jacob and Esau would see the same battle. Esau and Ishmael are the two fathers of the Arab nations and enmity still exists between the Arabs and Israel unto this day. The children of Israel in Egypt were persecuted and slaves for 400 years. Then the deliverer, Moses, came. You follow the history of Israel and see the same persecution over and over again. Every time the person who is going to be the next progenitor of Christ is known, he becomes the target of the enemy's attack. Finally Jesus is born. The enemy takes King Herod and motivates him to try to kill the Christ child, and we have what is known as the slaughter of the infants. The church has suffered under persecution throughout its history. These facts reveal the continuing enmity and hatred of the seed of the serpent for the seed of the woman.

The fact is that we are in a war with an enemy who is treacherous. There has also been a war by Satan on womanhood as a revenge for this verdict in the garden. He tried to make man think that women were cursed. In every society where the gospel

3

has not been influential, women are second-grade citizens unless they have by rebellion taken over and led that society. Wherever the gospel of Jesus Christ or the message of the Word of God has been proclaimed, women have been progressively liberated amongst those people. The women's liberation movement in America, properly understood, is another attack of the enemy on womanhood to destroy femininity. This war on womanhood is a vengeance against the channel for the Victor who would destroy the enemy.

This war against the seed of the woman continues in the New Testament. As soon as Christ began His public ministry in the wilderness, He was tested by the enemy. This testing continued throughout Christ's ministry—even through His own disciples. As Jesus was sharing about His coming journey to Calvary, Peter said, "Be it far from thee, Lord." Jesus responded by saying, "get thee behind me Satan." Paul refers to false apostles in the Scripture:

> For such are false apostles, deceitful workers, transforming themselves into the apostles of Christ. And no marvel; for Satan himself is transformed into an angel of light. Therefore it is no great thing if his ministers be transformed as the ministers of righteousness, whose end shall be according to their works. 2 Cor. 11:13-15

This passage reveals a satanic conspiracy: false apostles, angels appearing as light to deceive, to lead astray, to destroy, to bring man to disobedience to God.

In the Book of Revelation there is a key word, and that is "war." You cannot understand the Book of Revelation unless you understand that there is spiritual warfare going on. You see the satanic confederacy against God and His Christ unveiled. You find that the dragon warred against the saints (Rev. 13:7). God reveals a worldwide deception. The entire world, with few exceptions, goes for the antichrist kingdom. For this to happen, there must be a widespread preparation. Prophetic Scripture speaks of perilous times and deceiving, seducing spirits loosed upon the earth in the last days, which are loosed upon the earth even now:

> Now the Spirit speaketh expressly, that in the latter times some shall depart from the faith, giving heed to seducing spirits, and doctrines of devils. 1 Tim. 4:1

> This know also, that in the last days perilous times shall come. 2 Tim. 3:1

But of the times and the seasons, brethren, ye have no need that I write unto you. For yourselves know perfectly that the day of the Lord so cometh as a thief in the night. For when they shall say, Peace and safety; then sudden destruction cometh upon them, as travail upon a woman with child; and they shall not escape. But ye, brethren, are not in darkness, that that day should overtake you as a thief. Ye are all the children of light, and the children of the day: we are not of the night, nor of darkness. 1 Thess. 5:1-5

The Scriptures give us many signs of the times so that we can know that we are living at the end of the Church Age when these perilous times will come. If there has ever been a time when we have needed to understand spiritual warfare, it's now more than any time in the history of the church. Satan is in a relentless war against God, Jesus Christ and the church, but Christ has taken the victory.

When the fullness of time had come, God manifested Himself in the flesh in the person of Jesus Christ. He met this fallen archangel in mortal combat at Calvary and the Scripture says in Colossians 2:15 what the results of that combat were:

And having spoiled principalities and powers, he made a show of them openly, triumphing over them in it.

He took the victory at Calvary, and THERE IS A TOTAL AND COMPLETE VICTORY FOR EVERY CHRISTIAN OVER THE POWERS OF DARKNESS. The powers of darkness cannot rule in a Christian's life who understands how to stand and war in the Spirit. In order to stand and war in the Spirit, we have to get rid of deception. Satan was revealed a deceiver in the garden in the Old Testament, and as a deceiver throughout the New Testament. Deception is one of his major tactics. Deception exists on three planes. First is the plane of the unbeliever whom Satan keeps blinded to the reality of the gospel. Every unregenerate or unsaved person is deceived, according to the Scripture.

The heart is deceitful above all things, and desperately wicked: who can know it? Jer. 17:9

He feedeth on ashes: a deceived heart hath turned him aside, that he cannot deliver his soul, nor say, Is there not a lie in my right hand? Isa. 44:20

Exhort one another daily, while it is called To day; lest any of you be hardened through deceitfulness of sin. Heb. 3:13

In whom the god of this world hath blinded the minds of them which believe not, lest the light of the glorious gospel of Christ, who is the image of God, should shine unto them. 2 Cor. 4:4

Every unregenerate person in the world is deceived by sin and the wickedness of their own heart. They are blinded by the god of this world, by Satan and his emissaries. Wherefore, the Scripture says:

And you hath he quickened, who were dead in trespasses and sins: Wherein time past ye walked according to the course of this world, according to the prince of the power of the air, the spirit that now worketh in the children of disobedience. Eph. 2:1-2

First John tells us that the whole word lies under the control of the evil one. These are facts according to the Word of God. It should be alarming to us that deception is working so universally in our world.

The following are eight ways we are deceived. These apply to Christians as well as to the unsaved.

1. "Be ye doers of the Word and not hearers only, deceiving your own selves." James 1:22

2. "If any man among you seem to be religious, and bridleth not his tongue, but deceiveth his own heart, this man's religion is vain." James 1:26

3. "If we say that we have no sin, we deceive ourselves, and the truth is not in us." 1 John 1:8

4. "For if a man think himself to be something, when he is nothing, he deceiveth himself." Gal. 6:3

5. "Be not deceived; God is not mocked: for whatsoever a man soweth, that shall he also reap." Gal. 6:7

6. "Let no man deceive himself. If any man among you seemeth to be wise in this world, let him become a fool, that he may be wise." 1 Cor. 3:18

7. "Know ye not that the unrighteous shall not inherit the kingdom of God? Be not deceived, neither fornicators nor idolaters nor adulterers nor effeminate, nor abusers of themselves with mankind, Nor thieves nor covetous, nor drunkards, nor revilers, nor extortioners, shall inherit the kingdom of God." 1 Cor. 6:9

8. "Be not deceived: evil communications corrupt good manners." 1 Cor. 15:33

Be not deceived! If you fall into one of those categories, you shall *not* inherit the Kingdom of God. God's Word declares it. And if you think you can continue in some of those things and inherit the Kingdom of God, God's Word says you are deceived.

Evil communications corrupt good manners. You may say, "I don't like to tell my children whom they can have as friends." You have a responsibility, parents, to raise up your children in the way they should go and if the kids they are hanging out with continually bring out evil communication, be not deceived, they *will* corrupt good manners.

The chief weapon that Satan uses to keep the world in his power is *deception.* He likes to work in your relationships with deception; he likes to take the voice tones and twist them by the time they are heard by another. The enemy will twist and pervert in order to deceive you and plant suspicion. He wants to divide brethren. The Scripture says *mark them* who cause divisions among you.

I beseech you, brethren, mark them which cause divisions and offenses contrary to the doctrine which ye have learned and avoid them. for they that are such serve not our Lord Jesus Christ, but their own belly. Rom. 16:17, 18

Mark them, for they are not servants of God. That means they must be servants of the devil.

The unregenerate are deceived by sin. The enemy wants to keep them unsaved.

The second area of deception focuses on the carnal Christian, someone who is saved but who lives after the life flow of Adam instead of Christ, one who still lives in the flesh. He may not smoke, chew or run with those who do; he may not be getting drunk or fornicating, but he is still in the flesh and there is a whole set of deceptions to keep him there. A typical thought pattern for this kind of deception would be as follows: "You can't really overcome and live in the Spirit. That's just for special people; it was for the time of the apostles, but you have to live like you are. After all, none of us is really going to go on. Once you're saved, always saved, so you don't really have to change. You don't have to run the race to win, you don't have to press in to God, you can just sit back and say, I believe." However, the Bible says, "Thou doest well; the devils also believe, and tremble" (James 2:19). Hearers only deceive themselves. The object here is to keep one from going on to maturity.

There is a third level of deception, and that is subtle wiles of the devil for mature believers. There are those who have moved into a depth with God, have a degree of victory over their carnality, but now the enemy is working to keep them off guard, to overcome them in the spirit realm and render them ineffective.

Finally, my brethren, be strong in the Lord, and in the power of his might. Put on the whole armour of God that ye may be able to stand against the wiles of the devil. For we wrestle not against flesh and blood, but against principalities, against powers, against the rulers of the darkness of this world, against spiritual wickedness in high places. Wherefore take unto you the whole armour of God, that ye may be able to withstand in the evil day, and having done all, to stand.
Eph. 6:10-13

Our point here is that in the level of the believer's highest experience of union with the Lord we will find the keenest and the closest battle to be fought with the deceiver and his army. The most subtle, the most difficult battle is in the spiritual realm where you have the most intimate union with Christ. The enemy comes as an angel of light, or as the Christ, and you have to discern who he is. He comes very subtly, not with horns and a forked tail telling you to go out and rob a bank. Your real battles are on a level of such refined subtlety and sophistication that if you are going to rely on your ability, your understanding, and your discernment, you are going to fall flat. The only thing that can sustain you is the supernatural support of the Spirit of God, having taught you through the Word and having prepared you and tested you on levels of experience until there are built into you necessary characteristics that will cause you to be able to see and hear from God with safety. If you think you can get around this building process, you have made yourself a candidate for the deception of the enemy. You cannot succeed in warfare outside of God's patterns of safety in the church. The moment you think you can, you have opened yourself to the enemy and he will be sure to take advantage of it. He will get every inch out of you he can.

> Now the Spirit speaketh expressly, that in the latter times some shall depart from the faith, giving heed to seducing spirits, and doctrines of devils; Speaking lies in hypocrisy; having their conscience seared with a hot iron; Forbidding to marry, and commanding to abstain from meats, which God hath created to be received with thanksgiving of them which believe and know the truth. 1 Tim. 4:1-3

Some will fall away from the faith. Knowing we live in the latter times spoken of in the Scripture, I wonder which of you will be in this category. Some will fall away, not because of the failure of a church, nor because the pastor wasn't perfect, nor because someone did something wrong. The reason that some fall away is that they give heed to lying, seducing spirits of the devil.

Notice the nature of deception here, false doctrines of devils. Some prevalent phrases of false doctrine today are:

Whatever you say, you can have.

A Christian can be demon possessed.

You need to have someone assigned over you as your shepherd and you need to go to him with everything you do for permission and direction. (The Bible says there is *one* mediator between man and God and that is the man Christ Jesus.)

Just imagine Jesus coming to you in that hurt area of your life. (Jesus is a reality, not an imagination.)

Because some give heed to doctrines of devils, they fall away from the faith.

There are three basic ways that teaching spirits of the devil will seek to deceive us. One is a stream of Scripture text flowing through your mind, all out of context. For instance, someone was wondering about what they should do concerning a marital problem, opened the Bible, put their finger on a verse and it said, "Slay all of them: men, women and children. Spare none!" The devil brings Scripture to us out of context.

Another way the devil works is mixing the teaching of the Word with man's own reasoning, therefore coming to false conclusions. Paul said, "I dare not speak of any of those things that God has not wrought by me." What Paul taught was worked out in his life and proven, it wasn't his opinion. We need more than opinion; we need the Word of God.

A third way the devil works is to perpetuate false doctrines through deceived teachers. There is a difference between a deceived teacher and a false teacher. A deceived teacher may be teaching truth in one area and in another area be perpetuating a lie because he is deceived. There are many good men who teach the Word of God and do excellent jobs regarding salvation, but when they come to teach about the Baptism of the Holy Spirit, they are deceived. The effect of this ministry of deceiving, seducing spirits, according to this prophecy, is that the conscience is seared or cauterized, dulled and made unresponsive to truth. Therefore, it has a negative effect on your walk with God.

No one is above deception. One thing hit me and hit me hard when I got saved. I believed that I was on a path that would lead me to God and everything was going well because I was finding certain changes in my life and I was having dynamic experiences with spirit beings. When I got saved and came to know Jesus, I said in my heart as I knelt at that altar sobbing my way through to salvation, "I don't ever want to speak to anyone ever again about spiritual things. I don't want the responsibility." In my deception I influenced people into the kingdom of darkness, and I had to face that reality. As a result, I have a great respect for the fact that I can be deceived. I was so thoroughly deceived that when I woke up to the truth, I was in shock. Since then I have majored in trying to understand truth and God's Word and how to stay in a place of safety so that I would not be deceived again. I don't live with any fear, but I do live with a holy respect for the possibility of deception and take nothing for granted.

How do you test teaching? There are four things that wrong teaching will usually do:

1. It will weaken the authority of Scripture. The Word of God is both inerrant and infallible. The simplest way to confirm this is to ask the Lord Himself—if you know Him and His voice.

2. False teaching distorts the teaching of Scripture, twists it, or takes it out of context.

3. False teaching puts Scripture aside. Many teachers will build their doctrine off of subjective experience instead of the Word. I could take any particular behavioral or psychological experience that you could describe and begin to interpret it from the viewpoint of Freud, the humanist, EST, Henry Stack Sullivan, Adler, etc., and every viewpoint would be different and a complete system of interpolation and explanation for your behavior in itself. They can't *all* be true! This illustrates why *you*

cannot build doctrine on experience; it is subjective opinion. Doctrine must be built on the Word of God; wrong teaching will build off of some other foundation. The test, then, is harmony with the Word in the full body of truth, not one little section. One missionary puts it this way: If the doctrine will not stand up in every country and in every generation, it is not the Word of God.

4. False teaching often compromises the Cross and sin. For example, in Christian Science, spiritism, and new theology there is no sin, no saviour, no cross. In Islam, Confucianism and Buddhism there is no saviour, no cross. Christianity is unique in the world, the only religion that has an answer for sin.

The end result of this flood of deceiving spirits:

> Even him [antichrist], whose coming is after the working of Satan with all power and signs and lying wonders, And with all deceivableness of the unrighteousness in them that perish; because they received not the love of the truth, that they might be saved. And for this cause God shall send them strong delusion, that they should believe a lie: That they all might be damned who believed not the truth, but had pleasure in unrighteousness. 2 Thess. 2:9-12

This is the end of those who receive not the love of the truth, but receive the lie of deceiving spirits. Wherefore, John gives us a warning:

> Beloved, believe not every spirit, but try the spirits whether they are of God: because many false prophets are gone out into the world. Hereby know ye the Spirit of God: Every spirit that confesseth that Jesus Christ is come in the flesh is of God: And every spirit that confesseth not that Jesus Christ is come in the flesh is not of God: and this is that spirit of antichrist, whereof ye have heard that it should come; and even now already is it in the world. Ye are of God, little children, and have overcome them: because greater is he that is in you, than he that is in the world. They are of the world: therefore speak they of the world, and the world heareth them. We are of God: he that knoweth God heareth us; he that is not of God heareth not us. Hereby know we the spirit of truth, and the spirit of error. 1 John 4:1-6

This is a warning. Not every spiritual manifestation that comes along, even in the church, is to be received as from God. Try the spirit; learn to test and to judge.

The knowledge of truth, then, is the primary safeguard against deception. As you go to war, every area in which you are deceived will be an area where the enemy will throw his fiery darts at you. The enemy will use every area of deception as a stronghold; it will be like an armored tank, a fortress against you in battle.

The difficulty with deception is that you do not know it's not true; you believe it to be truth. *You must remain teachable.* As the Word of God is brought to you, truth will dawn; God will illuminate your mind and set you free.

The areas where you are deceived and where the enemy has had a stronghold worked in your life are points of difficulty in warfare. As you find truth established and worked into your life, you can stand in the face of the enemy in that particular area and you will be undaunted by his attack.

Father, we have learned that the enemy desires to deceive us so that we do not recognize the real warfare that is taking place. We also recognize that God not only wants us to become mature men and women of God overcoming the basic sins in our lives, but to be prepared warriors, soldiers in the Spirit, that we might war a good warfare for this generation. Remove every area of deception in our lives. Bring truth to us; set us free; and cause every stronghold of the enemy to be exposed and overthrown.

2

Satan, Who Is He?

Deception works on three planes. First, you have the unbeliever who Satan keeps blinded to the reality of the gospel. Second, you have the Christian who is immature and carnal, who lives in the natural man. The enemy deceives him in such a way that he lives in the flesh and in carnality instead of in the Spirit. The third plane is in the realm of walking by the Spirit. The enemy tries to overthrow us and render us ineffective.

Warfare doesn't actually begin until you enter that third realm. You might be the object over which warfare is battled in one of the other two realms, but you are not going to be able to battle well yourself. There is a distinction between the battle between the Spirit of God and the natural man and the battle between our spirit in the Lord versus the kingdom of darkness. Galatians tells us that the flesh wars against the Spirit and the Spirit against the flesh and that they are contrary so you cannot do the things that you would; but if you walk in the Spirit you will not fulfill the lusts of the flesh. This is a maturation problem and is not what we are talking about when we are talking about spiritual warfare. What is involved in true spiritual warfare is an invasion into an area where the enemy is ruling. By exercising the authority that we have in Christ we can overthrow Satan's particular sphere of influence according to God's purposes.

The best way to win a war is to know who your enemy is. If you don't know who you are fighting and if you don't know what makes them tick, you will have a hard time anticipating what they are going to do. The devil doesn't fight according to the rules. You must know what kind of enemy he is.

Let me illustrate. Elisha the prophet knew his enemy and King Joash of Israel did not. Elisha said, "Take this quiver of arrows and smite it on the ground." Joash smote the ground three times, and the prophet was wroth. He said, "You should have pounded it five or six times. You only smote the ground three times; therefore, the first three skirmishes with Syria you will win, but he will not be vanquished" (2 Kings 13). In other words, when you get the enemy down, finish him. If it's worth going to war over, do it right. You have to have the "killer's instinct" because the enemy is someone who will *never* show you mercy. He is someone who will *never* have any good designs on anything he does in your life.

Let us look at some Scriptures that will help us to understand what our enemy is really like. In Ezekiel 28 we have a prophecy of the judgment of God on the King of Tyre. In the middle of the prophecy there was a change of reference which begins in the eleventh verse, and it becomes quite clear that the person who is being spoken of cannot be an earthly personality. There is a law of double reference in the Scripture. According to this law, many times prophecy will refer to someone represented by the one spoken to. For example, the prophecy to Abraham of a promised child had an immediate reference to Isaac, but it also had a double reference to the real promised child which would come through Abraham's progeny over a period of generations, Jesus Christ. This law of double reference is in operation here in the twenty-eighth chapter of Ezekiel:

Moreover, the word of the Lord came unto me, saying, Son of man, take up a lamentation upon the king of Tyrus, and say unto him, Thus saith the Lord God: Thou sealest up the sum, full of wisdom, and perfect in beauty. Thou hast been in Eden the garden of God; every precious stone was thy covering, the sardius, topaz, and the diamond, the beryl, the onyx, and the jasper, the sapphire, the emerald, and the carbuncle, and gold: the workmanship of thy tabrets and of thy pipes was prepared in thee in the day that thou wast created. Thou art the anointed cherub that covereth; and I have set thee so: thou wast upon the holy mountain of God; thou hast walked up and down in the midst of the stones of fire. Thou wast perfect in thy ways from the day that thou wast created, till iniquity was found in thee. By the multitude of thy merchandise they have filled the midst of thee with violence, and thou hast sinned: therefore I will cast thee as profane out of the mountain of God: and I will destroy thee, O covering cherub, from the midst of the stones of fire. Thine heart was lifted up because of thy beauty, thou hast corrupted thy wisdom by reason of thy brightness: I will cast thee to the ground; I will lay thee before kings, that they may behold thee. Thou hast defiled thy sanctuaries by the multitude of thine iniquities, by the iniquity of thy traffick; therefore will I bring forth a fire from the midst of thee, it shall devour thee, and I will bring thee to ashes upon the earth in the sight of all them that behold thee. All they that know thee among the people shall be astonished at thee: thou shalt be a terror, and never shalt thou be any more. Ezek. 28:11-19

Ye are of your father the devil, and the lusts of your father you will do. He was a murderer from the beginning, and abode not in the truth. John 8:44

14

There was a point in time when the devil, formerly called Lucifer, turned away from truth. He had truth, he knew it, but he chose not to abide in truth. He was created in a very high and important position. We see from verse 12 that he was full of wisdom and perfect in beauty. Lucifer has been spoken of as an archangel or a special ministering spirit around the throne of heaven. In fact, there are three different individuals who are ministering spirits around the throne of God spoken of in the Scripture. One is Michael; in his functions and attitude he always carries out a message or task for the Father. Another one is Gabriel; he always carries out a message or function which parallels that of the Holy Spirit. The third one is Lucifer, who is the personification, or the spirit of antichrist that formerly carried out the task and expression of Christ before his fall.

Lucifer is described as being in the Garden of Eden. The garden which is pictured in Ezekiel 28 is a mineral garden full of precious stones. It was not a vegetable garden like the one that Adam and Eve were found in. We are looking here through the prophet's word at the time when Lucifer fell. Lucifer's fall was before the creation in seven days spoken of in Genesis 1, because in that creation Lucifer came in the person of the serpent and tempted Eve to disobedience. He was already fallen in that newly-created earth! Between Genesis 1:1 and 1:2 there was a great catastrophe. The Scripture says, "In the beginning God created the heaven and the earth. And the earth was without form and void; and darkness was upon the face of the deep. And the Spirit of God moved upon the face of the waters" (Gen. 1:1, 2). The remainder of the chapter speaks of the re-creation of the earth. In Isaiah 45:18 the scripture says that God did not create the earth without form and void. The phrase "in vain" (Hebrew *tohu*) is the same word that in Genesis 1:2 says the earth *was* (Hebrew "became") without form. Therefore, something happened. There was an original creation of the heavens and the earth and something cataclysmic happened which caused it to fall apart and to be without form and void. The Scripture implies that this event was the fall of Lucifer. There apparently was a heavenly Garden of Eden and there was an earthly Garden of Eden. The heavenly one was a garden that was filled with stones and it was a mineral-type of creation. The earthly was a vegetable garden with herbs, plants, and trees.

Lucifer, created as an archangel, had been in this mineral garden. What could that mineral garden really be? There is a parallel passage which speaks of the New Jerusalem to be created in the future at the end of the Millennium and one referring to God's throne.

15

And the foundations of the wall of the city were garnished with all manner of precious stones. The first foundation was jasper; the second, sapphire; the third, a chalcedony; the fourth, an emerald; the fifth, sardonyx; the sixth, sardius; the seventh, chrysolyte; the eighth, beryl; the ninth, a topaz; the tenth, a chrysoprasus; the eleventh, a jacinth; the twelfth, an amethyst. Rev. 21:19-20

Above the firmament that was over their heads was the likeness of a throne, as the appearance of a sapphire stone; and upon the likeness of the throne was the likeness as the appearance of a man above upon it. Ezek. 1:26

These passages describe a mineral creation like the garden that Lucifer was in. As an archangel, Lucifer ruled over a portion of creation. It says in verse 14 of Ezekiel 28, "Thou art the anointed cherub that covereth; and I have set thee so: thou wast upon the holy mountain of God." the holy mountain of God speaks of the governmental system of God. Lucifer, a special ministering spirit, full of wisdom and the sum of beauty, was between this mineral creation before the throne of god and the rest of creation in a place of leadership in the government of the kingdom of God. We see in verse 18 that not only was he a ruler, but he was a priest: "Thou hast defiled thy sanctuaries by the multitude of thine iniquities." We also find in verse 14 that he was the covering cherub, a particular priestly ministry of covering, or authority. The fact that Lucifer had sanctuaries indicates both worship and priesthood.

Lucifer was a ruler over a government; that is political in nature. He also had a priesthood, which indicates that he had a very important ruling ministry. The station of the cherubim that we saw in Ezekiel 1:26 is at the footstool of God's throne. This is also confirmed in Exodus 24:10 and 17. Verse 10 says that they saw the God of Israel and "there was under his feet as it were a paved work of a sapphire stone, and as it were the body of heaven in his clearness." Verse 17: "And the sight of the glory of the Lord was like devouring fire on the top of the mount in the eyes of the children of Israel."

Lucifer was not only in the Garden but he was down in the midst of the stones of fire. Examining what this description is in Ezekiel with other Scriptures indicates this garden is in the form of a mineral creation that is always in some way represented with the heavenlies, for the New Jerusalem is going to be the dwelling place of our Lord. There are pictures in the Old Testament of the heavenly throne room made of this mineral-type creation. We find that Lucifer was in this mineral creation as the anointed cherub. The place of the cherub was by the throne room, or the footstool of God's throne. He functioned as a ruler in God's Kingdom with a priestly ministry to God and the creation. He stood between God and creation; his authority was derived from God and was worked through him by God. During the time that he was perfect there was only one will in the universe, and that was the will of God. There had never been rebellion against God in the history of eternity. **IN ETERNITY THERE IS NEVER ANY WILL BUT THAT OF GOD.** In the realm that we call time there is more than one will.

Lucifer was ruling in the holy mountain of God; he was an anointed cherub, a priest, full of wisdom and beauty. His innermost being was created as music. It says, "the workmanship of thy tabrets and of thy pipes was prepared in thee in the day that thou wast created."

He was reflecting christ, as Michael reflected the Father and Gabriel reflected the Holy Spirit. Then in Hebrews we learn that our Lord, who Lucifer was reflecting, is a songleader!

I will declare thy name unto my brethren, in the midst of the church will I sing praise unto thee. Heb. 2:12

This Scripture is quotation of a prophecy of Christ as a songleader in the church. Good song-leading ministry bringing worship unto the father is the ministry of Christ. The antichrist, Lucifer, was a great songleader, a great musician with tremendous musical ability created in him. One of his functions was to lead that portion of creation with which he worked, in worship unto God. *Is it any marvel, then, that one of the major tools that the enemy uses in this day and from the beginning of the fall of man is music? Is it any marvel, then, that there is a spiritual anointing from the devil on music in the world?* He perverts the worship of God. Music was created for worship and music that is not used in worship is a perversion of God's intention. Music which is designed for anything other than to glorify God is something lower than that for which it was created (cf Rev. 4:11).

"Thou wast perfect in thy ways from the day that thou wast created till iniquity was found in thee." The word "iniquity" means: lawless, not willing to come under law, wanting to be independent from God, not willing to be under God's authority or to be accountable to Him. I don't know how many times we can see that in the Scripture and then turn around as Christians and justify a life without accountability in the Kingdom of God,

17

without accountability in the church, without accountability for the ministry that we seek to perform in His name. If we are going to have any ministry in the name of the Lord, we must be accountable to God. Lucifer said, "I don't want to be accountable. I don't want to be under God's authority. I'm beautiful; I'm perfect; I've got all this authority and I can do my own thing independent from God." That is iniquity, the foundation of sin.

Is it any wonder, then, that in spiritual warfare the enemy will seek to get you to do the same thing? Isn't that what happened in the fall in the Garden? Adam and Eve were to follow God's will and they were to live a spiritual life sustained by doing the Word of God (as our physical life is sustained by the food we eat). The enemy encouraged them to go against God's Word and to eat from the Tree of the Knowledge of Good and Evil. He was saying, "You can develop your created life and you can live this abundance without being dependent on God." The other option was to obey the commandment of the Lord, partake of the Tree of Life and develop a life of dependency and sharing in the life of the Creator. the enemy's intent is to sever the dependency and bring an independence from God in all that we do.

> By the multitude of thy merchandise they have filled the midst of thee with violence, and thou hast sinned. Ezek. 28:16

Merchandise here is not a reference to being a merchant or retail salesman. Let me illustrate the meaning of this word. Take a politician, for example, who is on a committee for defense. He knows that they are going to give a contract to make so many war planes to a particular company and the stocks are low. He goes out and says, "Get me $100,000 under the table and a free stock option of so much and I will be sure that you get the contract." This is merchandising, *taking advantage of our position for personal gain at the expense of others.*

Lucifer, who was in this position, having passed through his hands the authority of God to the creation and the worship of the creation to God, made merchandise. He began to take unto himself some of the authority, praise, worship, honor, and credit that belonged only to God, and he made merchandise of God's authority and God's honor.

Wherefore, the Scripture says in 1 Timothy 3:6 that one of the qualifications of those who will be an overseer in the house of God is "Not a novice, lest being lifted up with pride he fall into the condemnation of the devil." A novice is one who does not have a proven ministry. He has learned a few things, has a few answers, a few gifts, a little anointing, and a little fruit. Often a novice wants to be independent from the body, without any accountability to the governmental structure in the body. (But you have no ministry without accountability because there is no such thing as authority without accountability.) He says, "I am submitted to God but I am submitted to no man. I'll submit directly to the Lord but I'll not submit to a man." Jesus said, "In that you have done it unto the least one of these, my brethren, you have done it unto me." We find a heart of rebellion and iniquity in wanting to be independent from God.

An unproven ministry without proper preparation may find a few gifts operating with a few results. He may fall into the trap of taking unto himself that which should be given to God, and he's made merchandise of the ministry.

On the other hand, he turns around and gets a little authority and seeks to use it for his own gain. This is making merchandise of God's authority, and that is what Lucifer did. He had a place of priestly and governmental authority; he had a place of being used of the Lord; he took to himself the honor and authority that belonged to God and he made merchandise of them. Therefore, God said, "I will cast thee down; thou hast profaned and defiled thy sanctuary."

The enemy in warfare wants to catch you in one of those traps. Some of you are hungry for God to use you more, but God in His mercy is withholding certain gifts of the Spirit and a certain measure of His anointing from your life because He knows your heart. He knows that if He gave you that anointing and those gifts, your head would get so puffed up that you would be caught in this merchandising trap of the devil and you would lose your soul in hell because you wouldn't be able to handle the anointing. GOD, WHO VALUES YOU MORE THAN WHAT HE CAN ACCOMPLISH THROUGH YOU, WITHHOLDS THAT ENABLEMENT UNTIL YOUR CHARACTER QUALIFIES YOU.

I am kind of a domineering, forceful type of person, and as a new Christian God was using me and I wanted to get out and do something for Him. There were some things in my life that weren't right but that didn't bother me. The Lord would take care of them. Let's go for it. A dear brother came and put his arm around me and said, "I have no concern about the ministry God is going to give you. He has shown me He has wonderful things in store for you, but I'm concerned about your safety." Safety? What does that mean? That brother loved me enough to talk to me about some areas that needed healing and development, priorities to be adjusted, and the Lord began to work. That was the beginning of an orientation that I have been growing in from that day forward, to be more interested in the person than what function the person can perform.

Unfortunately, many people are more interested in what they can get out of a person than they are in that person's genuine welfare, because the enemy has worked in this area. However, that is changing. God is speaking in this hour about relationships, and character and righteousness being implemented in our lives. Priorities are being adjusted. But the enemy has this as a foundation of his own heart: *HE MADE MERCHANDISE OF THE THINGS THAT GOD HAD GIVEN HIM, TOOK THEM UNTO HIMSELF AND AS A RESULT, HE FELL.* He wants to get us in the same trap that he is in.

> How art thou fallen from heaven, O Lucifer, son of the morning! how art thou cut down to the ground, which didst weaken the nations! For thou hast said in thine heart, I will ascend into heaven, I will exalt my throne above the stars of God: I will sit also upon the mount of the congregation, in the sides of the north! I will ascend above the heights of the clouds; I will be like the most High. Yet thou shalt be brought down to hell, to the sides of the pit. Isa. 14:12-15

What happens when the creation challenges God's right to rule? It is a question of authority. *All sin in essence is a question of authority.*

How do we relate to that authority? Wrong authority is one thing; right authority is another. That is why it is so important to establish your authority as a parent over your children, to teach them how to properly relate to authority, and that you do not misuse authority and foster rebellion. One way that God can establish authority is by force, but that destroys love relationships. Love by its very essence has to be voluntary. Wives submit to their husbands because they love them; submission is a love word. Jesus said, "If you love me, keep my commandments." Obedience is a love word, and when authority does not work on the basis of love, relationship is broken. If you love, there is submission.

Why can you submit to God? When you know He loves you, you can trust Him. When He wins your heart, you can open up without reservation and surrender all that you are, all that you have, all that you will ever be to Him without any hesitation, because you *know* His love for you and you trust Him. Not only do you trust His heart and His intention, but you learn to trust

His capability of carrying that intention out. Sometimes you find a fellow human who you know has the best of intentions but if you trust him, you're going to be in trouble because he has no capacity to carry out that intention. People ask, "Why is there so much sin and suffering in the world?" God allows that and puts up with it because He is working in suffering to reach man so he can voluntarily choose to receive His love instead of having to take the forceful consequences of rebellion.

There are five "I will's" in this Scripture. First Lucifer says, "I will ascend into heaven." He must have been ruling on earth in the old creation. Stop and think about what's happening here. I imagine that the Godhead was involved in a council one day and decided, "Let us make a creation like unto us. Let us make man in our image." That doesn't mean that we were to look like God. But there were certain capacities and characteristics that we were to have that are like unto God which would give us the capability of a voluntary love relationship with God and of being one with Him in all of His fullness so that the Creator could share the essence of His being with us, a special creation. Lucifer says, "*I* will sit also upon the mount of the congregation on the sides of the north; *I* will ascend to the heights of the clouds; I, I, I will be like the most High!"

But that is what *we are* going to be. "For whom he did foreknow, he also did predestinate to be conformed to the image of his Son" (Rom. 8:29). We are going to be like the most High by being partakers of His life. That was not Lucifer's option. Here we see another attitude of his. You have seen it when a couple of kids get together: "Well, if I can't be quarterback than I'm going to take my football and go home." "If I don't have it my way, then I'm going to take all my toys and you can just stand there and look at yourself." That's Lucifer! How many of us have that attitude?

You will never be fulfilled except in the place that God has created for you. You can't be like someone else. You *can* be like Jesus—in the capacity that He has ordained for you. The unwillingness to accept who you are or what you are is this attitude of Lucifer. The enemy perverts, brings rebellion towards what we are, and the world culture develops a fad of idols and you want to be like them instead of who you are: dress like them, look like them, walk like them, act like them, do what they do, and never be who you really are. We should enjoy our uniqueness!

Satan was going to exalt himself, break rank, not stay in the position that God gave him. One of the hardest things to do is play second fiddle but sometimes God puts you in a place where you have to do just that. Normally, the person playing first fiddle gets all of the credit or attention and you don't get any, and that is hard because we all like to be in the limelight. The way to get a person happy in a conversation is to talk about him. But not everyone is called to be a David, and there are many people like Jonathan who love God as much as David did, who have the anointing of God and the power of God, who have the natural position, but God says, "Lay it all down for this fellow over here," and because they love God enough they do so willingly, eagerly, without reservation, and commit themselves in the face of all opposition to support God's choice.

The inability to do that was another characteristic of the heart of Lucifer. He fell from pride; he was going to exalt himself. In so doing, by breaking rank, he was seeking to be independent from God. Pride comes before a fall (Prov. 16:18). "I beheld Satan as lightning fall from heaven" (Luke 10:18).

If we are going to be effective in warfare, we must know who our enemy is. We have seen something about who he was, his nature, what he was created for, the position he occupied, what was in his heart that made him fall, making merchandise of God's authority and honor. He fell into a trap because he wanted to be independent from God and came out from under God's authority, accountability and lordship. He wanted to break rank because he wanted to be like some other creation. That means he was seeking satisfaction in himself and who he was as opposed to finding his satisfaction in God. IF HE HAD FOUND SATISFACTION IN GOD, IT WOULD NOT HAVE MATTERED WHAT PLACEMENT GOD PUT HIM IN, BECAUSE HIS PLACEMENT WOULD NOT HAVE BEEN THE SOURCE OF HIS SATISFACTION.

There is no redemption for Lucifer, *ever*. He is as thoroughly evil as God is good, and he is your enemy. He has a confederacy of demons and they are working in this world against you. You are his target. His nature with music, his attitudes, his positions, his ministry, his wanting authority, honor and glory, to be independent and self-exalting, his wanting to be like another, all are foundational to his character and therefore become foundational to what he does against you in warfare. Watch for these subtleties because your sin nature is in harmony with these attitudes of the enemy, the seeds of them lie in every one of us. Except the Cross of Calvary is applied and we allow the Spirit of God to deal with our natural man that we might abide in the Spirit, we will be in that same trap. That is why we have need for patterns of safety; we should have enough sense not to put any trust in our own flesh.

Father, we are wanting to understand who our enemy is and how he works so that we can be effective in warfare. Not only that we can triumph within our own lives but that we can be effective soldiers, channels through whom you can release those who are in bondage in this world. The seeds of rebellion have been in our fallen nature. How we thank You, God, for your provision on Calvary, not only to be cleansed and forgiven but to be set free. Lord, there is not one of us with an honest heart who doesn't recognize that within our flesh there is no good thing; that is, within our natural man, that all that is good within us is because your life was birthed in us at the miracle of salvation and your life is growing and maturing in us and our character is being formed so that we can learn how to walk with You and abide in You. I'm asking that if some of the areas that have been exposed in Lucifer are running unchecked in any reader's heart, by your Holy Spirit You would bring it to their awareness and help them to bring it into submission to You, committing it into your hands to be broken, to be reigned and ruled and overcome. Amen.

3

The Activities of Satan

There are seven main areas where we find the activity of Satan. The first one is as **TEMPTER**. Satan is one who wants to bring temptation. We must balance this with James, who tells us that we are tempted when we are drawn away by our own lusts or desires; we cannot blame the devil for that. However, when the enemy is active in us as a tempter, he brings something to us to stimulate a fallen desire and to try to get us involved in it, whether it be pride, unbelief, fear, covetousness, lust, or whatever. We find in John 14:30 that on the night Christ was betrayed, He was sharing with His disciples:

Hereafter I will not talk much with you: for the prince of this world cometh and hath nothing in me.

As the enemy would come to test and to tempt the Christ in the night He would be betrayed, Jesus said, "he has nothing in me." That is a place where we all need to be. If there is a love of the world in our hearts, if there is a love of things that are ungodly, then we cannot say that the enemy has nothing in us. When he comes to tempt, he always searches out and finds that area where we have a love of the world or of the things that are outside the priorities of God, and that is the area where he begins to tempt us, to stimulate and entice us.

Defraud ye not one the other, except it be with consent for a time, that ye may give yourselves to fasting and prayer; and come together again, that Satan tempt you not for your incontinency. 1 Cor. 7:5

We see in this situation that when desires of the natural are strong and stimulated, the enemy wants to draw us aside, to tempt us.

We know that whosoever is born of God sinneth not, but he that is begotten of God keepeth himself, and that wicked one toucheth him not. 1 John 5:18

We must keep ourselves from sin. He will come to you to entice you, to tempt and seduce you. "seduce" means to lead astray. Remember what he did in the fall of man—first he called into question the Word of God: "Hath God said ... ?" Then he flattered: "Don't you see that these things will cause you to be like God? It's something good." Then he contradicted God's Word: "You will *not* surely die." He led astray.

The second area where Satan works is in the area of **REBELLION AGAINST DIVINE AUTHORITY**, of which he is the originator. In 1 John 3:8, the Scripture says that Christ was manifested that He might destroy the works of the devil, which includes rebellion.

In Ephesians 2:2 we learn something about the course of this world and how the enemy is working in terms of rebellion against God's authority.

In time past ye walked according to the course of this world, according to the prince of the power of the air, the spirit that now worketh in the children of disobedience.

Every unsaved person walks in a direction, lives in a lifestyle, and in a social consciousness that was originated, stimulated, and developed by rebellion, the spirit that works in disobedience.

The Kingdom of God is never really advanced by power, it is advanced by divine authority. The power is what backs up the authority. The question of sin is really a question of authority. Does God have the right to rule? Is He Lord or is something else lord in our lives? If we choose against the will of God, that is defined in the Scripture as sin. As the enemy has worked in America, we have seen such an attack on the authority structures of our society in terms of our governmental leaders, our law enforcement, and the authority structure in the home. There is a satanic attack on authority to pervert it or discredit it in our lives.

The third area in which Satan works is **DECEPTION** which is where his greatest power lies. Jesus talked about how there would be false Christs, false apostles; many will be deceived. The word "deceived" means to believe something to be true that is in fact a lie. It is not a question of sincerity. One of the mores that the devil has placed in our society is that, If we are sincere, it is okay. Sincerity is not enough; there must be truth.

If what you believe is in fact a lie, then you are living in deception and that has eternal consequences. There is a common deception in our culture set by the devil to block the preaching of the gospel of Jesus Christ, when God has given us a commandment to preach the gospel to every creature. The deception says, "Don't press your belief because others have a right to believe what they want and you are not tolerant." This is a lie of the devil, yet there are many Christians who accept it and live by it. Just because you are a Christian does not make you free from the deception of the devil! Deception will lead you to hell or ineffectiveness. Its purpose is to keep you out of the will of God.

Some people, because they get involved in spiritism and occultism, have an experience and say, "It's real." Of course it's real. Every Christian knows the devil is real. The Scripture says, "Even the devils believe and tremble." Uri Geller can make a spoon bend. Does that or a table levitating help the blind or crippled or a family torn apart by adultery and divorce? Lies are reality, they exist; but, you must understand them for what they are. To misunderstand them is to be deceived.

The fourth area in which the enemy works is **ACCUSATION**.

And the Lord said unto Satan, Hast thou considered my servant Job, that there is none like him in the earth, a perfect and an upright man, one that feareth God, and escheweth evil? Then Satan answered the Lord, and said, Doth Job fear God for nought? Hast not thou made an hedge about him, and about his house, and about all that he hath on every side? thou hast blessed the work of his hands, and his substance is increased in the land. But put forth thine hand now, and touch all that he hath, and he will curse thee to thy face. Job 1:8-11

Satan said that the only reason Job served God was because He blessed him, that if there wasn't any blessing he wouldn't serve God. In other words, we don't serve truth because it is true, we serve truth because it feels good, it causes me to do better, or I have more money in my pocket and a nicer house. That may be true for some people, but it wasn't for Job. Satan accused him, and he accuses every Christian he can find.

The Christian hypocrite is another accusing lie of the devil. By definition there is no such thing as a Christian hypocrite. If one is a genuine hypocrite, then he is not a Christian. That is like saying, "There goes a Christian devil!" Jesus said, "You will know them by their fruit. A good tree does not bring forth corrupt fruit, and a corrupt tree does not bring good fruit" (cf Matt. 7:17-20). If there is good fruit coming from a tree, then it is alive, it is Christian. But if it has corrupt fruit, that is hypocrisy and is not Christian.

And he showed me Joshua the high priest standing before the angel of the Lord, and Satan standing at his right hand to resist him. And the Lord said unto Satan, The Lord rebuke thee, O Satan; even the Lord that hath chosen Jerusalem rebuke thee: is not this a brand plucked out of the fire? Zech. 3:1-2

Satan is there to resist and accuse:

Now is come salvation, and strength, and the kingdom of our God, and the power of his Christ: for the accuser of our brethren is cast down, which accused them before our God day and night. Rev. 12:10

There is no condemnation to those who are in Christ Jesus, who walk after the Spirit and not after the flesh. You are a new creation. The Scripture says of a genuine Christian that his sins have been washed in the Blood, *never* again to be remembered against him and to be removed from him as far as the east is from the west. You go to pray for a need, and Satan says, "You can't believe God. Remember what you did the other day? On your way to work you slammed the door, gave your wife that hit-and-run kiss good-bye, and you kicked the dog. Now God can't answer your prayer." Every time you go to pray, the accuser brings up before the Lord all the little things that aren't exactly as you would like them to be. You may have them under the Blood, you may have sought forgiveness and repented, but he accuses. Not only does he accuse you, but he accuses others. "Do you know what brother so-and-so said about you?" He creates suspicion. That is why the Bible speaks against gossip.

Another area where the enemy works is **AFFLICTION,** both physical and mental.

And lest I should be exalted above measure through the abundance of the revelations, there was given to me a thorn in the flesh, the messenger of Satan to buffet me, lest I should be exalted above measure. 2 Cor. 12:7

And ought not this woman, being a daughter of Abraham, whom Satan hath bound, lo, these eighteen years, be loosed from this bond on the sabbath day? Luke 13:16

The sixth area is **OPPOSITION.** He wars against the Kingdom and against God. Acts 10:38 tells us Jesus went about healing all those that were oppressed. "Wherefore we would have come unto you, even I Paul, once and again; but Satan hindered us" (1 Thess. 2:18). Paul and company tried to go to Thessalonica to minister to the body of believers there, but Satan hindered them and they didn't make it.

"Be sober, be vigilant; because your adversary the devil, as a roaring lion, walketh about, seeking whom he may devour" (1 Peter 5:8). We are as sheep, and the lion always goes after the straggler, the weak one who is sick or injured or who can't quite keep up, or the young, the babe who doesn't know how to defend itself or keep up with the herd: the easy target. Our adversary, the devil, is like a roaring lion, walking and stalking the flock seeking whom he may devour.

This is why when new Christians come in, it is so important that they be nurtured and helped until they grow and become established. That is why when you know that someone is going through a hard place, it is so important to contact them, to support them in prayer and in love, and to encourage them. A person may be sick for a couple of weeks. If no one seems to visit or call or be concerned, the devil comes to that person and says, "They don't care about you. Nobody loves you." He begins to attack, seeking whom he may devour. It is our responsibility to make sure that doesn't happen in our fellowship. You *are* your brother's keeper.

When Satan fell, "his tail drew the third part of the stars of heaven, and did cast them to the earth: and the dragon stood before the woman which was ready to be delivered, for to devour her child as soon as it was born" (Rev. 12:4). He opposed everything that was of God. The devil will not bother you as long as you are not furthering the Kingdom of God because you aren't going to be causing him any trouble. As soon as you start to do something for the Kingdom of God, there will be a special emissary of the devil assigned to you to stop it. We are in a war, and it should be no surprise that there is opposition.

The seventh area is **DEATH.**

Michael, the archangel, when contending with the devil, disputed about the body of Moses, durst not bring against him a railing accusation, but said, The Lord rebuke thee. Jude 9

Forasmuch then as the children are partakers of flesh and blood, he also himself likewise took part of the same; that through death he might destroy him that had the power of death, that is the devil, and deliver them who through fear of death were all their lifetime subject to bondage. Heb. 2:14, 15

Even Christians, because they have not gotten over the fear of death, are subject to bondage of the devil. Fear is not of God; He has not given us a spirit of fear but a spirit of love and of power and a sound mind.

When ministering in India, I was told by nationals in certain cities that what I was doing would bring my life into a very dangerous position. In Poona, the Hindus brought two hundred hired nationals to storm the platform and to seek my life. The police commissioner wanted to close the meeting, but God helped us to talk him out of it. When the nationals saw those two hundred hired people on the grounds, they were so afraid that not one would sit on the platform and not one would work with the crowd. But I knew the Lord would give us total and complete victory, and He did. After the crusade was over, the man who hired these people came to apologize to me saying he knew I was a man of God. I asked him how he knew this. He replied, "When I gave the signal to storm the platform, not one of those two hundred people was able to lift their arms!" God sovereignly intervened.

After Christ died on Calvary and rose again, He had the keys to death, hell, and the grave in His hand. For a non-Christian there is not the protection that there is for a Christian. The non-Christian is still living according to the course of this world, the prince of the power of the air, and Satan is at work in him. But God sovereignly has the keys of death and hell in His own hand. The devil cannot take your life anymore than he could take Christ's life.

If you will learn these seven areas in which the enemy works, it will help you when you go to war spiritually. You know who your enemy is, what his character and nature are like; that he wants the glory, honor and authority which belongs to God for himself. He can't be just a channel because that which is channeled through him he wants to take unto himself.

Have you ever had a similar desire in your own heart? Money is channeled and there is a temptation to embezzle; honor is channeled and there is a temptation to want to take a little to yourself; privilege is channeled and you want to take some of that for your own end. These are areas where Satan will seek to overthrow you.

Father, I ask that You will help every reader to be sensitive to You in these seven areas of attack. Build them in your Spirit to be strong and fortified in these areas so that they may stand strong in the power of your might to war a good warfare and to glorify your name.

4

Satan's Counterfeit

Man is religious by nature because God created man to worship Him. If man does not worship the true and living God by the power of the Holy Spirit, then he will often resort to a counterfeit, worshiping the god of this world with the help of evil spirits. There are many kinds of counterfeits, some obvious and some subtle.

Satan has a throne as God has a throne. Jesus speaks of this in Revelation 2:13. Satan has a throne; therefore, he has a kingdom over which he rules.

Satan has doctrines. "Now the Spirit speaketh expressly, that in the latter times some shall depart from the faith, giving heed to seducing spirits, and doctrines of devils" (1 Tim. 4:1). Examples of devilish doctrines: "All paths lead to God." "You get married, you ruin the relationship; just live together." "Abstain from meats." "The day of miracles is passed." "You can't believe the whole Bible because it is culturally biased." "You can have the Baptism of the Holy Spirit without speaking in other tongues." "You need to have someone to talk to who will help you mature and who will disciple you and can confirm everything you do or don't do and we'll assign this one to you to raise you up; he will serve as a mediator between you and God." The Bible says there is only one mediator between man and God and that is the man Christ Jesus (1 Tim. 2:5).

Revelation 2:9 speaks of the synagogue of Satan; that means he has a temple. First Corinthians 10:21 speaks of the communion table of devils: "Ye cannot drink the cup of the Lord and the cup of devils: ye cannot be partakers of the Lord's table, and of the table of devils." Verse 20 of that same chapter speaks of the devil's sacrifice: "But I say that the things that the Gentiles sacrifice, they sacrifice to devils and not to God: and I would not that ye should have fellowship with devils."

And no marvel; for Satan himself is transformed into an angel of light. Therefore it is no great thing if his ministers be transformed as the ministers of righteousness. 2 Cor. 11:14, 15

Not only is Satan as an angel of light, which is false light because he is the king of darkness, but his messengers come to us as either demons or men. He has his own ministers. One of the more sophisticated forms of pastors in the devil's kingdom are psychiatrists. There are Christians in that field, few and far between, but as a whole the profession has been built upon doctrines of devils.

If Satan cast out Satan, he is divided against himself; how shall then his kingdom stand? Matt. 12:26

Satan has a kingdom. Revelation 16:14 speaks of counterfeit miracles, signs and wonders. "For they are the spirits of devils, working miracles, which go forth unto the kings of the earth and of the whole world, to gather them to the battle of that great day of God Almighty." When Moses was going to lead Israel out of Egypt, the magicians in the courts of Egypt imitated the first three signs that he did. They could cast their rod down and it became a serpent just as Moses' rod. *There are lying miracles of the devil!* There are false apostles and prophets and teachers.

But there were false prophets also among the people, even as there shall be false teachers among you, who privately shall bring in damnable heresies, even denying the Lord that bought them and bring upon themselves swift destruction. 2 Peter 2:1

And in Matthew 13:38 Jesus warned of false apostles.
We have the New Jerusalem, which is the City of God, the Bride of Christ, but there is also Mystery Babylon.

Upon her forehead was the name written, MYSTERY, BABYLON THE GREAT, THE MOTHER OF HAR-LOTS, AND ABOMINATIONS OF THE EARTH. Rev. 17:5

Satan seeks to be worshiped, which you see in the temptation of Jesus. There are false Christs who have gone out into the earth. John says in 1 John 2:18-22 that even now there are antichrists in the earth. In Revelation 13 we see an imitation of the Trinity, for you have the great beast which is the counterpart to the Father, you have the antichrist and you have the false prophet.

There are several areas in which Satan is working. He will produce the antichrist in the political realm. Because we are at the end of the age, the political realm is now being groomed for the antichrist to arise. There is also the false prophet who arises and is spoken of here as an antitype of the Holy Spirit. The reason we see such a revival of spiritism and occultism is to develop the knowledge of darkness to bring forth the false prophet. First Timothy 3:16 speaks of the mystery of godliness, which is the ability of God to reproduce Himself in you. Second Thessalonians 2:7 speaks of the mystery of iniquity, which is the ability of the enemy to reproduce himself in you and which is already at work in the earth today.

And after the sop Satan entered into him. Then said Jesus unto him, That thou doest do quickly. John 13:27

What? know ye not that your body is the temple of the Holy Ghost which is in you, which ye have of God, and you are not your own? 1 Cor. 6:19

Demon spirits want to possess your body. As a genuine Christian you can never be *possessed* except by God, but you can be *oppressed,* opposed, and afflicted by the devil. There is a difference between being afflicted by the enemy and being possessed by him.

Satan not only has his seven areas where he works, but he has his counterfeit religion and he wants to bring us into his belief system. The Book of Revelation reveals that as the antichrist comes to power, the false prophet is going to lead people to bow down and worship him.

God has permitted sin to reign and run its course as a witness to its destructive fruit, but there is a seven-fold judgment of Satan:

1. When Satan sinned, he was cast out of Paradise in the third heaven, which is the presence of God. "Yet thou shalt be brought down to hell, to the sides of the pit" (Isa. 14:15).

By the multitude of thy merchandise they have filled the midst of thee with violence, and thou hast sinned: therefore, I will cast thee as profane out of the mountain of God: and I will destroy thee, O covering cherub, from the midst of the stones of fire. Ezek. 28:16

Jesus later spoke as the disciples came back from healing the sick and casting out devils, "I beheld Satan fall as lightning from the heavens."

2. He was judged in Eden at the fall of man. God spoke a judgment against him and he is under an irrevocable curse of God.

32   And the Lord God said unto the serpent, Because thou hast

done this, thou art cursed above all cattle, and above every beast of the field; upon thy belly shall thou go, and dust shall thou eat all the days of thy life: And I will put enmity between thee and the woman and between thy seed and her seed; it shall bruise thy head and thou shalt bruise his heel. Gen. 3:14, 15

3. He was conquered at Calvary by Christ.

The Son of God was manifested, that he might destroy the works of the devil. 1 John 3:8

Now is the judgment of this world: now shall the prince of this world be cast out. John 12:31

[The Holy Spirit will come to convince] Of judgment, because the prince of this world is judged. John 16:11

4. The devil and his hosts are being conquered by the church as the Body of Christ releases the captives of the human race. Wherefore, these signs will follow them who believe: they shall cast out devils (Mark 16:15-20). The commission of the Apostle Paul was, "To open their eyes [the Gentiles], and to turn them from darkness to light, and from the power of Satan unto God, that they may receive forgiveness of sins, and inheritance among them which are sanctified by faith" (Acts 26:18). You and I have a commission to carry out that judgment on the devil and to release the captive humanity.

5. Satan and his angels are to be cast out of heaven and into the earth at the close of this age. It will be a result of the man child arising; it will be a result of the principalities and powers being overcome. We find in Revelation 12 that as the man child is born, there is a war in heaven and Michael and his archangels battle and travail with the dragon. That old serpent called Satan who deceives the whole world is cast out into the earth and his angels are cast out with him. At that point in time we hear the cry, "Now is come salvation, and strength, and the kingdom of our God and the power of his Christ, for the accuser of our brethren is cast down."

Who is the man child? Some people say that the woman is Israel and the man child is Christ, but Christ was not caught up to heaven immediately when He was born, neither was Israel immediately sent into the wilderness at the ascension of Christ. Therefore, it is not a picture of Israel and Christ. Some say that it

33

is the church born out of Israel, but the church wasn't really born out of Israel; also, we don't find that the church was caught up into heaven immediately after it was born. But this is what we do see: The woman is a representative of all of the people of every generation who are right with God, seeking to bring forth to completion a company of people who will come into full maturity in their relationship with a redemptive Christ. This is the man child who will be birthed at the end of the age, and that man child will actually take his authority as a child of God and cast down the powers of darkness.

The only place in the Scripture where we see Satan falling as lightning besides this one in Revelation 12 is when Jesus commented on the result of what He saw when the seventy brethren who he ordained had gone out into the cities to preach the gospel, cast out devils, and heal the sick. They came back rejoicing, saying the devils were subject to them, and Christ said, "I beheld Satan as lightning fall from heaven" (Luke 10:18). The Scripture uses the image of Satan as lightning falling from heaven as a picture of the authority of the believer in Christ taking dominion over the powers of darkness.

6. He will be cast out of the earth into a bottomless pit for a thousand years at the Second Coming of Christ.

And he laid hold on the dragon, that old serpent, which is the Devil, and Satan, and bound him a thousand years; And cast him into the bottomless pit, and shut him up, and set a seal upon him, that he should deceive the nations no more, till the thousand years should be fulfilled: and after that he must be loosed a little season. Rev. 20:2, 3

7. The final judgment is the Lake of Fire.

And the devil that deceived them was cast into the lake of fire and brimstone, where the beast and the false prophet are, and shall be tormented day and night for ever and ever. Rev. 20:10

This will be for all the host of Satan and all men who choose to serve Satan in this life.

EVIL SPIRITS

Satan is not omnipresent, and the majority of the time when believers are saying, "Get behind me, Satan" they are talking to a demon and not to Satan. Satan is at the top of the kingdom of darkness, but the majority of the time you are not dealing with Satan. In dealing with the kingdom of darkness, you are mainly dealing with spirits that are under Satan's authority, demons that harass, hinder, and put up opposition.

What are evil spirits? What do we know about them from the Scripture? What are their general realms of activity? If we are going to be involved in spiritual warfare, in dealing with the powers of darkness, we need to know about demons and evil spirits. We need to recognize that under Satan's control is a vast army of evil spirits that are very committed and very loyal to him. In Scripture they are called fallen angels, authorities, principalities, powers, rulers of darkness, wicked spirits, demons; all of these titles would suggest that there are ranks and levels of authority in Satan's kingdom.

Fallen angels

> He cast upon them the fierceness of his anger, wrath, and indignation, and trouble, by sending evil angels among them. Ps. 78:49

The word "angel" literally means messenger and is applied in many ways in the Scripture.

> And there was war in heaven: Michael and his angels fought against the dragon; and the dragon fought and his angels; And prevailed not; neither was their place found any more in heaven. And the great dragon was cast out, that old serpent, called the Devil, and Satan, which deceiveth the whole world: he was cast out into the earth, and his angels were cast out with him. Rev. 12:7-9

There are angelic types of beings who are following Satan. We also find in Romans 8:38, 39 things that will not separate us from the love of Christ:

> For I am persuaded, that neither death, nor life, nor angels, nor principalities, nor powers, nor things present, nor things to come . . . shall be able to separate us from the love of God.

Obviously, those angels are not God's servants if they are trying to separate us from God, so by implication this speaks of evil angelic beings oriented to an anti-God attitude and posture in the anti-God kingdom, the kingdom of darkness.

It is evident that when Satan fell, a vast company of angels fell with him (Rev. 12:4); possibly it was one-third of the angels which fell. "His tail drew the third part of the stars of heaven, and did cast them to the earth." Stars of heaven are often spoken of in the Scripture as a symbol for angelic beings.

We understand that there are three individuals in the Bible known as archangels: Gabriel, who is always expressed as having a ministry which is parallel to that of the Holy Spirit; Michael, whose ministry is always parallel to that of the Father; and Lucifer, the fallen angel who is now called Satan, the spirit of antichrist. When you see a third of the stars of heaven fall, and you know there are fallen angels who followed after Satan, you can conclude that most likely one-third of the angels were under the command of each one of these archangels and those who were under the command of Satan followed him. That is only an assumption, but we do have evidence that there were angelic beings who fell following Satan. These angels aren't all in the same category.

> If God spared not the angels that sinned, but cast them down to hell, and delivered them into chains of darkness, to be reserved unto judgment; 2 Peter 2:4

The word "hell" here is *Tartarus*. We find that angels who sinned in a certain way were cast down into this place spoken of as Tartarus.

> The angels which kept not their first estate, but left their own habitation, he hath reserved in everlasting chains under darkness unto the judgment of the great day. Jude 6

We find here a group of angels who are chained in darkness somewhere until the day of judgment. Some angels are bound in various parts of the earth, and others are loose.

> Saying to the sixth angel which had the trumpet, Loose the four angels which are bound in the great river Euphrates. And the four angels were loosed, which were prepared for an hour, and a day, and a month, and a year, for to slay the third part of men. Rev. 9:14, 15

Some angels are able to appear as angels of light.

> For such are false apostles, deceitful workers, transforming themselves into the apostles of Christ. And no marvel; for

Satan himself is transformed into an angel of light. 2 Cor. 11:13, 14

Satan's ministers are formed as ministers of righteousness whose end will be according to their works. They will eventually be cast out of heaven, and you and I as Christians, in a certain hour appointed by God, will be in a place of judging them.

Know ye not that we shall judge angels? how much more things that pertain to this life? 1 Cor. 6:3

We see that the devil and his angels will be cast into the lake of fire in a final judgment.

Then shall he say also unto them on the left hand, Depart from me, ye cursed, into everlasting fire, prepared for the devil and his angels. Matt. 25:41

Demon spirits

There are three theories about the origination of demon spirits. One is that the angels who fell with Satan are demons. Some say that demons are disembodied spirits of a pre-Adamic life on earth; we find that when God created man, He told him to *re*plenish the earth. The third theory is that they are the spirits of the unnatural offspring of angels. God did not make the origin of demon spirits clear in His Word, but He does reveal that they are real personalities who are able to think, act, and speak, and they especially desire to express themselves through mankind.

An apparent difference between demons and fallen angels seems to be that fallen angels do not seek to inhabit a human body; nowhere do we see that effort by a fallen angel in the Scripture. However, we do see demon spirits trying to inhabit the human body. It is even possible for them to inhabit animal bodies and to express their destructive nature.

[The demons] cried out, saying, What have we to do with thee, Jesus, thou Son of God? art thou come hither to torment us before the time? And there was a good way off from them an herd of many swine feeding. So the devils besought him, saying, If thou cast us out, suffer us to go away into the herd of swine. And he said unto them, Go. And when they were come out, they went into the herd of swine: and behold, the whole herd of swine ran violently down a steep place into the sea, and perished in the water. Matt. 8:29-32

The following is the only instance of Satan himself ever entering into a person that we know of:

> And after the sop Satan entered into him [Judas]. Then said Jesus unto him, That thou doest, do quickly. John 13:27

In Mark 5:1-20, we find Jesus talking to the demon spirits, asking them what their name was. Many trying to deal with demons ask them what kind of spirit they are and what their name is. Jesus can do that, but you should not seek knowledge from demons because they aren't a very reliable source! If you want to find out what kind of a spirit it is, ask the Lord who is omniscient and knows all things; you can count on what He has to say!

The two words most often used in the New Testament referring to demons are either "devils" or "spirits." The Greek word *daimon* is translated "devil" in many places; the Greek word *pneuma* is translated "spirit." So we find that demons are spirits. It should be remembered that there is only one devil; the rest are demon spirits or fallen angels and these spirits are under Satan's control.

Demon spirits have all the characteristics of a personality; they possess will, intelligence, and they act according to their evil natures. This is evident as these demons ask Jesus, "Why have you come to us? Have you come to torment us before the appointed time?" They knew of an appointed time of judgment. They recognized the Son of God when all He did was walk by, and they said, "Be nice to us. Don't send us to that place yet. Let us go into the swine."

They also have a belief system. "Thou believest that there is one God; thou doest well: the devils also believe, and tremble" (James 2:19). James was writing to people who confessed Christianity but did not walk with God, who continued to live without bringing their lives under the lordship of Christ and allowing God to change them. If you are not in the process of continually being changed, something is wrong with your Christianity. The only exception would be if you were perfectly in the likeness and image of Christ; otherwise, if you are rightly related to God, you are in the process of being changed!

Demons are spirit beings. As a result, they are incorporeal, invisible, and although they often manifest their nature and character in human beings, they are still spirits.

Demons are Satan's servants. Having chosen to side with

Satan in his rebellion, they became his slaves, obligated to do his bidding. Thus, the choice they made was really Satan's and through self-will they became slaves to his will.

Then was brought unto him [Jesus] one possessed with a devil, blind and dumb: and he healed him, insomuch that the blind and dumb both spoke and saw. And all the people were amazed, and said, Is not this the son of David? But when the Pharisees heard it, they said, This fellow doth not cast out devils but by Beelzebub the prince of the devils. And Jesus knew their thoughts, and said unto them, Every kingdom divided against itself is brought to desolation; and every city or house divided against itself shall not stand: And if Satan cast out Satan, he is divided against himself; how shall then his kingdom stand? And if I by Beelzebub cast out devils, by whom do your children cast them out? therefore they shall be your judges. But if I cast out devils by the spirit of God, then the kingdom of God is come unto you. Or else how can one enter into a strong man's house, and spoil his goods, except he first bind the strong man? and then he will spoil his house. He that is not with me is against me; and he that gathereth not with me scattereth abroad. Matt. 12:22-30

We recognize here by the intimation of Jesus that these demon spirits are servants of Satan. They are loyal to Satan, they are not divided in that house; there is a unity of will, of purpose, of direction.

They are numerous. On one occasion a demon admitted to Jesus that his name was Legion, "for we are many." As God has legions of good angels at His command, so Satan has legions of demon spirits at his. You hear of people who get involved in certain kinds of demonic activity having auditory hallucinations and hearing the buzzing of the Lord of the Flies. Sometimes it sounds like a conversation that you can't quite make out.

As God and His Kingdom are known by symbols in the Scripture, so Satan and his hosts are symbolized by various things. Each symbol will bring out an aspect of their nature. We have eagles as a spiritual nature, the ox as a servant nature, the lamb as Christ; they symbolize aspects of the things of God. So it is that symbols of demon spirits teach us something about their nature.

PICTURES OF EVIL SPIRITS

Scavenger Birds

> And after these things I saw another angel come down from heaven, having great power; and the earth was lightened with his glory. And he cried mightily with a strong voice, saying, Babylon the great is fallen, is fallen, and is become the habitation of devils, and the hold of every foul spirit, and a cage of every unclean and hateful bird. Rev. 18:1, 2

An unclean bird in the Hebrew vernacular is a scavenger, a dirty old buzzard who likes to eat the dirty, rotten filth of the earth. That is a picture of a demon spirit.

Frogs: slimey, living in the dark regions.

> And I saw three unclean spirits like frogs come out of the mouth of the dragon, and out of the mouth of the beast, and out of the mouth of the false prophet. For they are the spirits of devils, working miracles, which go forth unto the kings of the earth and of the whole world, to gather them to the battle of that great day of God Almighty. Rev. 16:13, 14

Locusts and Scorpions

> And he opened the bottomless pit; and there arose a smoke out of the pit, as the smoke of a great furnace; and the sun and the air were darkened by reason of the smoke of the pit. And there came out of the smoke locusts upon the earth: and unto them was given power, as the scorpions of the earth have power. Rev. 9:2, 3

> The shapes of the locusts were like unto horses prepared unto battle; and on their heads were as it were crowns like gold, and their faces were as the faces of men. And they had hair as the hair of women, and their teeth were as the teeth of lions. And they had breastplates, as it were breastplates of iron; and the sound of their wings was as the sound of chariots of many horses running to battle. And they had tails like unto scorpions, and there were stings in their tails; and their power was to hurt men five months. Rev. 9:7-10

Serpents and Vipers

> Then said he to the multitude that came forth to be baptized of him, O generation of vipers, who hath warned you to flee from the wrath to come? Luke 3:7

There are many different kinds of demon spirits under satanic control and their names signify their evil works. Demons are totally, morally depraved in character, though there seem to be degrees of wickedness in them (Matt. 12:22-30).

Names of demons: Devils, evil spirits, servants of the devil; unclean spirits (describing their impure nature); dumb spirits (unable to speak); blind and dumb spirits; deaf and dumb spirits; foul spirits; lying spirits; the spirit of infirmity; spirits of divination (fortune telling); seducing spirits (religious spirits which bring false doctrines and doctrines of devils); lunatic spirits (epileptic and suicidal); anti-Christ spirits; spirit of boredom; spirit of the world; spirit of error; spirit of fear; perverse spirits; familiar spirits (sensual, like a spirit of prostitution, knowing).

The activity of demon spirits as servants of Satan is best summed up in John 10:10: "The thief cometh not, but for to steal, and to kill and to destroy." These spirits attack mankind spiritually, morally, mentally, physically, and emotionally.

Things That Demons Do Under Satan's Control

1. They oppose God's ministers.

When any one heareth the word of the kingdom, and understandeth it not, then cometh the wicked one, and catcheth away that which was sown in his heart. Matt. 13:19

This is opposition to the Kingdom of God, the ministry of the Word. As the Word of God is being ministered, if you don't understand it, a demon spirit will come and oppose it and try to snatch it out of your heart. That is why we need to be sure our heart is right with God when we come to church. ONE REASON A PERSON DOESN'T UNDERSTAND GOD'S WORD IS BECAUSE HIS HEART ISN'T RIGHT TOWARDS GOD! In every service God will talk to you if your heart is right towards Him, and if that isn't happening, it is a good indication that there is something wrong between you and the Lord.

You must have ears to hear. Whom does God open understanding to but those whose hearts are towards Him? Demon spirits will lie to you and keep you bound in Christian religion without reality of relationship with God. That is why you don't understand the Word at times.

I remember a woman who once came to me who, every time you turned around, God was "telling her" to do this and to do

41

that. She had a Christian husband who was living in another apartment who hadn't been in adultery, who wanted to have the relationship right and who was seeking counseling. She just decided that she didn't like his mannerisms and didn't want to live with him. I finally told her, "Don't tell me that God told you this or God told you that. If God was telling you anything and you were able to hear, you would hear Him say be reconciled with your husband. And until you hear that message, everything else that you are calling God is either self or a demon spirit!" God says that He will not receive your gift until you go and be reconciled with your brethren (Matt. 5:23-24).

2. Demons pervert the Word of God and seek to hinder the gospel. Wherefore, we would have come unto you but Satan hindered us. 1 Thess. 2:18
   Now the Spirit speaketh expressly, that in the latter times some shall depart from the faith, giving heed to seducing spirits, and doctrines of devils. 1 Tim. 4:1

3. They ensnare their captives. They are tenacious, they don't want to let them go.

Moreover, he must have a good report of them which are without; lest he fall into reproach and the snare of the devil [speaking of a bishop]. 1 Tim. 3:7
And that they may recover themselves out of the snare of the devil, who are taken captive by him at his will. 2 Tim. 2:26

4. They blind the minds of unbelievers.

In whom the god of this world hath blinded the minds of them which believe not, lest the light of the glorious gospel of Christ, who is the image of God, should shine unto them. 2 Cor. 4:4

When you are witnessing to unbelievers, one of the things you must do to be effective is to take dominion over the spirit of the enemy which is blinding their understanding, because you are dealing with demonic power that is holding them in blindness.

5. They sow tares among the wheat. That means there are false believers and in your heart are false concepts from demons.

The field is the world; the good seed are the children of the kingdom; but the tares are the children of the wicked one; The enemy that sowed them is the devil; the harvest is the end of the world; and the reapers are the angels. Matt 13:38-39

6. They seduce people. The Greek word *planao*, translated "seduce," means they rove as tramps and by implication are imposters and misleaders. They seek to draw aside from the path, to lead astray, to allure, to corrupt, to defraud, or to entice. A seducing spirit can cause people to be obsessed with a false idea or doctrinal imbalance.

7. They inject thoughts. The battleground of spiritual warfare is in the mind.

For though we walk in the flesh, we do not war after the flesh: (For the weapons of our warfare are not carnal, but mighty through God to the pulling down of strong holds;) Casting down imaginations, and every high thing that exalteth itself against the knowledge of God, and bringing into captivity every thought to the obedience of Christ. 2 Cor. 10:3-5

8. They trouble people.

But the spirit of the Lord departed from Saul, and an evil spirit from the Lord troubled him. 1 Sam. 16:14

God allowed an evil spirit to trouble Saul as judgment in his life. The Hebrew word for "troubled" (*bâ'ath*) means to make fearful, afraid, to terrify. Many people going through "depression" who are suddenly terrified are dealing with a demon spirit. It speaks of agitation of mind, perplexities, and uneasiness.

So Saul died for his transgression which he committed against the Lord, even against the word of the Lord, which he kept not, and also for asking counsel of one that had a familiar spirit, to inquire of it; and inquired not of the Lord; therefore he slew him, and turned the kingdom unto David the son of Jesse. 1 Chron. 10:13, 14

He was perplexed, uneasy, and the spirit that he followed led him to his death and eternal destruction.

9. They oppress people.

How God anointed Jesus of Nazareth with the Holy Ghost and with power: who went about doing good, and healing all that were oppressed of the devil; for God was with him. Acts 10:38

The Greek word for "oppress" (*katadunasteuo*) means to exercise dominion against, overburden in mind or body, to have a domination.

10. They also vex people.

And, behold, a woman of Canaan came out of the same coasts, and cried unto him, saying, Have mercy on me, O Lord, thou son of David; my daughter is grievously vexed with a devil. Matt. 15:22

Lord, have mercy on my son: for he is lunatick, and sore vexed: for ofttimes he falleth into the fire, and oft into the water. Matt. 17:15

The Greek words for vex (*pascho; daimonizomai*) carry the following meanings: It involves a person experiencing sensations or impressions, usually in such a way that it causes discomfort in terms of their feelings, passions, and suffering. The word "vex" also means to mob, to harass or to molest, to suffer at the hands of another, to have auditory and visual hallucinations, harassments, pain, emotional startling of different kinds, physical problems.

11. They also bind people.

And ought not this woman, being a daughter of Abraham, whom Satan hath bound, lo, these eighteen years, be loosed from this bond on the sabbath day? Luke 13:16

In the Greek, the word "bound" (*deo*) means to tie up, confine, fasten as with cords. It should be recognized that although physical infirmities may be caused by demons, it does not mean that every case fitting one of these descriptions is demonically inspired, but it does tell you that demons do these kinds of things!

12. They deceive people:

And Jesus answered and said unto them, Take heed that no man deceive you. For many shall come in my name, saying, I am Christ; and shall deceive many. Matt. 24:4, 5

And many false prophets shall rise, and shall deceive many. Matt. 24:11

For there shall arise false Christs, and false prophets, and shall show great signs and wonders; insomuch that, if it were possible, they shall deceive the very elect. Matt. 24:24

And the great dragon was cast out, that old serpent, called the Devil, and Satan, which deceiveth the whole world: he was cast out into the earth, and his angels were cast out with him. Rev. 12:9

13. They possess people.

When the even was come, they brought unto him many that were possessed with devils: and he cast out the spirits with his word, and healed all that were sick. Matt. 8:16

And when he was come to the other side into the country of the Gergesenes, there met him two possessed with devils, coming out of the tombs, exceeding fierce, so that no man might pass by that way. Matt. 8:28

As they went out, behold, they brought to him a dumb man possessed with a devil. Matt. 9:32

Possession (Greek, *diamonizomai*) denotes both the occupancy and ownership of a person by an evil spirit, an indwelling control. Possession means to be under the power and control of a demon who has entered a person and can control his faculties at will. Cases of possession in the Bible caused lunacy, palsy, dumbness, blindness, enabled fortune telling, and they resist being unclothed from a human body.

No truly born-again believer, as long as he is still in a saved condition, can be possessed by demons because the Holy Spirit dwells within the believer's spirit and the Bible says that he who is joined to the Lord is one Spirit (1 Cor. 6:17). If your spirit is one with the Lord's, how can a demon control it? That doesn't mean that as a Christian you can't be harassed or oppressed or have certain bondages, but it does mean that you are not under the domination and control of their will. Demons mainly lead the Christian by deception, and through their deception they cause the believer to yield to them.

14. They torment people; their torment is like the tormenting sting of a locust (Rev. 9).

15. They buffet people (2 Cor. 12:7). To buffet (Greek, *kolaphizo*) means to hit with blow after blow, to punch, to slap, and to fight against. Have you ever been in the position of going forward with the Lord and every time you take a step forward to take the victory for a city or county of your family, you get a blow here and a blow there? That is a buffet from Satan and Christians face them all the time. When that is happening at a time you are pressing forward into God, it is a good confirmation that you are doing something worthwhile because the devil won't resist **nothing!** If you are not doing something to disturb his kingdom, he is not going to hassle you but he will give you strokes because he wants to encourage you in that which doesn't disturb his scheme of things.

16. Demons resist people.

And he shewed me Joshua the high priest standing before the angel of the Lord, and Satan standing at his right hand to resist him. And the Lord said unto Satan, The Lord rebuke thee, O Satan; even the Lord that hath chosen Jerusalem rebuke thee: is not this a brand plucked out of the fire? Now Joshua was clothed with filthy garments, and stood before the angel. Zech. 3:1-3

Demons oppose, stand up against, and act as an adversary to us.

On demons, judgment is progressive and culminates at the same time as Satan's in the lake of fire. They are conquered and spoiled at Calvary (Col. 2:15) and are made subject to Christ (1 Peter 3:22).

Spiritual warfare is *not* dealing so much with your flesh. The Bible says in Galatians 5 that the Spirit wars against the flesh and the flesh against the Spirit so that you cannot do the things that you would. This is a war with the carnal nature not yielding to the Spirit of God. There is a world of difference betwen our struggle with our rebellious nature against God's Spirit and the struggle of the Kingdom of God in the power of His Christ against the kingdom of darkness. They aren't totally unrelated because if the devil can get you in the flesh, he knows that you will not be effective in the Spirit against him. He will be content for you to be a Christian as long as you do nothing to disturb his kingdom. *If you aren't disturbing Satan's kingdom, then you are not all that God wants you to be. You will not be allowed to continue that way because God will disturb your present to improve your future!*

Once you learn to understand and see after the Spirit, you will recognize demonic activity. You don't have to be afraid of demons, but you do have to deal with them. The person who ignores them is in trouble, because when you ignore them you are playing ostrich and allowing them to do their own thing unhindered.

When you go to war, you must be someone who will run the Christian race. Paul said he kept his body in subjection lest he, having preached the gospel to others, would himself be a castaway. He said we don't fight as ones who beat the air; you must have your target, you must be prepared. That is why a good boxer, even though he may not have superior strength or stamina, can outfight someone who is not a boxer because the boxer will know how to set a person up and lay him out. That is what you must do in your war against the enemy.

Father, help us to understand and be sensitive to your Spirit in dealing with demonic activity in our world. Teach us of your victory and how we can meaningfully take the victory on behalf of those who are bound. Amen.

5

The Victory of Christ

Every victory that we will experience, every means by which we are able to gain victory in spiritual warfare, anything ever accomplished or received in the Kingdom of God, finds its foundation and source in the victory of the Lord Jesus Christ on Calvary. In conquering Satan and all of his emissaries, demonic hosts, and fallen angels, Christ has made complete victory available to every believer. It doesn't matter what area you struggle in, you need to know that Christ's victory on Calvary is enough to have a provision available to you for total and complete victory in your life. Do you have a problem you are struggling with? Do you have an area in which you battle the enemy? Do you have difficulty standing in the victory of Christ? Think of what that area may be and take a moment to look around in the Body of Christ. See if you can find someone who gained a victory over your kind of problem, and you will. Paul said some were effeminate, some were thieves, some were embezzlers, some were murderers, some were adulterers—*were*, they are no longer (1 Cor. 6:9, 10). Ask them how they got the victory, and they will point you to Calvary. Christ's victory is enough for every believer to have total victory.

That doesn't mean you are born with it as you get saved. The Bible says that as many as received Him, to them gave He power or ability to become the sons of God (John 1:12). "Sons of God" in the Scripture is a phrase that speaks of spiritual maturation. A born-again believer has the power or ability to *become* victorious. This requires development and growth. A person like me will never be a great opera singer. It doesn't matter how much I practice, it doesn't matter who taught me, it doesn't matter what kind of lessons I have. You must have it on the inside; you either have it or you don't. Some people do more with the 10 percent they have than some do with the 90 percent they have, but when you get down to it, you must have the ability. The Bible says that if you have received Christ, He gave you the ability to become. What are you going to do with it?

Christ, because of His victory on Calvary, has become Lord of all principalities and over all powers.

Therefore, will I divide him a portion with the great, and he shall divide the spoil with the strong; because he has poured out his soul unto death; and he was numbered with the transgressors; and he bore the sin of many, and made intercession for the transgressors. Isa. 53:12

Why would He have the spoils? Because He took the victory on Calvary. How is that manifest?

Then was brought unto him one possessed with a devil, blind, and dumb; and he healed him, insomuch that the blind and dumb both spake and saw. And all the people were amazed, and said, Is not this the son of David? But when the Pharisees heard it, they said, This fellow doth not cast out devils, but by Beelzebub the prince of the devils. And Jesus knew their thoughts, and said unto them, Every kingdom divided against itself is brought to desolation; and every city or house divided against itself shall not stand: And if Satan cast out Satan, he is divided against himself; how shall then his kingdom stand? And if I by Beelzebub cast out devils, by whom do your children cast them out? therefore they shall be your judges. But if I cast out devils by the Spirit of God, then the kingdom of God is come unto you. Or else how can one enter into a strong man's house, and spoil his goods, except he first bind the strong man? and then he will spoil his house. He that is not with me is against me; and he that gathereth not with me scattereth abroad. Matt. 12:22-30

A man by demon possession was blind, deaf and dumb and Jesus healed him. He told His accusers that He did it by binding the one who was ruling in that house and casting him out. He had authority over the demon.

The victory of Christ can be seen in three major parts: His life, His death, and His resurrection. Christ overcame Satan personally in the wilderness and representatively for us at Calvary.

Love not the world, neither the things that are in the world. If any man love the world, the love of the Father is not in him. For all that is in the world, *the lust of the flesh, and the lust of the eyes, and the pride of life* is not of the Father but is of the world. 1 John 2:15, 16 (italics mine)

This speaks of the wrong uses of body (lust of the flesh), soul (lust of the eyes), and spirit (pride of life), the three major dimensions of our being. It was this kind of test in which Jesus found Himself in Luke 4. He came to this test as the last Adam, or the second Man. Adam was tested in three realms. When Adam fell, he

49

brought all of his unborn race under satanic control and into the kingdom of sin, sickness, and death. Because Christ overcame, we have deliverance from that kingdom.

To understand Christ's temptation, we need to see it in the context of the first Adam, as Christ was spoken of as the last Adam.

> The serpent was more subtle than any beast of the field which the Lord God had made. And he said unto the woman, Yea hath God said, Ye shall not eat of every tree of the garden? Gen. 3:1

He began by questioning God's Word.

> And the woman said unto the serpent, We may eat of the fruit of the trees of the garden: But of the fruit of the tree which is in the midst of the garden, God hath said, Ye shall not eat of it, neither shall ye touch it, lest ye die. Gen. 3:2, 3

God did not say they couldn't touch it, and He did say that if they ate it they would *surely* die, not *lest* they die. By questioning God's Word, there already begins to be a compromise.

> The serpent said unto the woman, Ye shall not surely die: For God doth know that in the day ye eat thereof, then your eyes shall be opened, and ye shall be as gods, knowing good and evil. And when the woman saw that the tree was good for food [lust of the eyes], and a tree to be desired to make one wise [the pride of life], she took of the fruit thereof, and did eat, and gave also unto her husband with her; and he did eat. Gen. 3:4-6.

Satan tempted Adam and Christ in a way that you and I are never tempted. That temptation came totally from without, because Adam was made innocent. He did not find himself on the earth with a sin nature. He was created neither holy nor evil; he was in a state of innocence, and his choices to God's commands and God's authority would determine whether it would be holiness or evil. Christ's temptation, because He was 100 percent man and 100 percent God, was also not from within but was from without. We are tempted from within as well as from without; we are drawn away by the lust of our own flesh. We see the three elements spoken of in 1 John that we will see in the test of Jesus.

The lust of the flesh is one area in which Satan works to exploit

the five basic laws of our physical nature: (1) the law of self-preservation; (2) self-acquisition; (3) self-sustenance; (4) self-propagation; (5) self-assertion. Without a sense of self-preservation, we would walk off a cliff. Without a sense of acquisition, we wouldn't build anything. Without sustenance, we wouldn't develop and grow crops to maintain ourselves. Without propagation, the species would die. Without self-assertion, we would never subdue and have dominion over the earth as God commanded man from the day he was created.

There is nothing wrong with these appetites of the flesh, they were God-given. But the lust of the flesh is an exploitation of one or more of these appetites to place these desires above the authority of God. That is the difference between lust and love. Love is giving; lust is seeking for ourselves beyond the boundaries that God has given us, putting our own selfish desires above God's authority.

All of this was an area where the enemy was trying to bring man's will into submission to himself as opposed to submission to God. There are two kinds of freedom: one is freedom from sin where you are in submission to God's authority; the other is freedom from righteousness where you are in submission to Satan's authority. There is no middle ground. There is the kingdom of light or the kingdom of darkness. Jesus said, "If you are not gathering with Me, then you are scattering abroad. If you are not for Me, then you are against Me." There is no place of neutrality with the things of God.

When we go to war, the enemy will attack us in these three arenas: body, soul, and spirit. The body is the sense realm. We have a desire sometimes to live in the sense and appetite realm above the authority of God.

> Being forty days tempted of the devil. And in those days he did eat nothing: and when they were ended, he afterward hungered. And the devil said unto him, If thou be the Son of God, command this stone that it be made bread. And Jesus answered him, saying, It is written, That man shall not live by bread alone, but by every word of God. Luke 4:2-4

If you have fasted for three days, five days, or two weeks, you know that one thing which happens when your fast is over is you hunger. Christ hungered after forty days; he did not eat or drink. It was a supernatural fast. The devil came to Him and said, "Use your authority. If You are really the Son of God, You can turn that stone into bread by your word. Feed your flesh and satisfy your hunger." The temptation was to take what He had and use it for selfish purposes outside of God's authority. Jesus said, "No, it

51

is written: Man will not live by bread alone, that which sustains our body, but by every word of God, that which sustains our Spirit, the essence of our life." In referring to His ministry, Jesus said, "I do nothing of myself, but what I see my Father do" (John 5:19). He would not act supernaturally out of selfish motivation but only in submission to His heavenly Father. This temptation was to use that authority for His own selfish physical gratification outside of God's authority.

Every time you are tested in the physical realm, this is the essence of the test. Are you going to take the sexual appetite, are you going to take that desire for food, are you going to take that desire for things, for power and recognition, are you going to take that desire to preserve yourself and exercise it beyond God's authority? Or are you going to keep it in submission to the authority of God?

Jesus passed that test. Then Satan decided to test Him in the realm of soul, which is the area of mind, will, and emotions.

> And the devil, taking him up into an high mountain, showed unto him all the kingdoms of the world in a moment of time. And the devil said unto him, All this power will I give thee; and the glory of them: for that is delivered unto me; and to whomsoever I will I give it. If thou therefore wilt worship me, all shall be thine. And Jesus answered and said unto him, Get thee behind me, Satan; for it is written, Thou shalt worship the Lord thy God, and him only shalt thou serve. Luke 4:5-8

He took Him in a moment of time and showed Him all the kingdoms of this world in a test of the soul. This was an attempt to exploit the desires for self-assertion, to subdue and have dominion. Jesus overcame it once again with the Word of God.

You will be tempted in certain areas of your life which will stimulate your affections for the wrong things, which will stimulate your intellect and your mind the wrong way, which will go after your will to bring it into captivity to things of the devil—through deception, illusion, and leading astray.

Satan finally tested Jesus in the Spirit.

> And he brought him to Jerusalem, and set him on a pinnacle of the temple, and said unto him, If thou be the Son of God, cast thyself down from here: For it is written, He shall give his angels charge over thee, to keep thee: And in their hands they shall bare thee up, lest at any time thou dash thy foot against a stone. Luke 4:9-11

Satan knows Scripture and he is using it here, but notice how he uses it. If you go back to Psalm 91:11, which he is quoting, you will find that he left out the phrase, "to keep thee *in all thy ways,*" thereby twisting the meaning. He takes it out of context, leaves out a phrase, and twists the meaning and tempts Jesus to use His power for Himself to demonstrate who He was in response to Satan's challenge and not the Father's leading. Jesus said, "I can of my own self do nothing." He was in submission to the Father. When He became a man, He became obedient, even unto the death of the Cross.

Our spirit is the place where we commune with God. You don't commune with God in your mind, with your emotions or your will. You *respond* to God with your will, you *understand* God in your mind, you have emotional affection towards God, but you *commune* with God in your spirit. You know intuitively by the revelation of His Spirit in your spirit. Your conscience (the function to approve or disprove actions) works in your spirit, not out of your mind. In your mind you can understand all of the religious systems in the world to the point where you can explain them even better than some of the priests, but your intellectualism will in no way tell you which one is truth, because the carnal mind is enmity against God.

The natural man cannot know the things of God because they are spiritually discerned. You must know God after the Spirit. The Bible says the Word of God divides asunder between the soul and the spirit showing the thoughts and intents of the heart. How can you see your spirit? In your attitude, your intentions, and motivations; these reflect your spirit.

Christ was being tested in His spirit to see if He would use a motivation or intention that was not from the Father and act out of Himself instead of out of the Father. Remember Lucifer's fall—it had to do with the fact that he wanted to be independent of God. But Jesus would not act outside of the Father's authority or outside of His leading.

As an example of this, I had a neighbor who was a psychiatrist and during the time we were having our Miracle Services at the Civic Center, he wanted me to go to a leukemia ward where he worked to clean out all the sick from their beds. I said, "If it was under my control, that is probably exactly what I would do, but that is just why it is not under my control. I have to be a worker together with God, according to His purposes." Do you know how much damage we would do because of our lack of understanding, our lack of knowledge, our lack of discretion, our wrong response to what happens? Look at what we have done with everything we have received anyway. Haven't we misused it in some ways? *The important things of life, spiritual truth and reality, are yet held under the control of God the Father and never really come under the control of man!* Later, my psychiatrist neighbor became a Christian.

He himself hath suffered being tempted, he is able to succour them that are tempted. Heb. 2:18

For we have not an high priest which cannot be touched with the feeling of our infirmities; but was in all points tempted like as we are, yet without sin. Heb. 4:15

In principle, Christ was tested in every area that you and I can be tested. He overcame and was without sin. He overcame personally to prepare a life that could be deposited in you that would be found incorruptible, that couldn't be overthrown by anything that hell or Satan and all his demons could throw at you, that would be so pure, so strong and undefilable that you couldn't help but overcome! *Aren't you glad that He didn't just give you forgiveness, but that He gave you life that is incorruptible, undefeatable, that can't be defiled, that is pure and clean and will not bend to the power of darkness under any circumstance?* This is just the beginning of His ministry demonstrating the kind of life that is in you by the new birth.

Jesus was tempted in every point. You say, "Well, He doesn't understand my problem. I was traumatized by this mean, demon-possessed man when I was a little child. Christ doesn't understand what it means to be forsaken of God. He doesn't understand what it is like to be beaten, ridiculed, and mocked." Go back and read about the Cross of Calvary. He knows rejection when innocent; He knows mockery; He knows persecution; He knows physical defilement; He knows what it is to be spat upon; and He knows what it is like in that moment to have His Father's face turned from Him because of divine purpose. He knows *every* thing that you can experience and has provided a way of fulfillment, overcoming, victory, and healing for your life!

He overcame in the wilderness by the Word of God. When you go to war you won't be able to use your three-dimensional technicolor vision that God may have given you, all the goosebumps or all the times you were slain in the Spirit. They won't be worth anything in the midst of the battle. When you get into the battle, you must have your feet planted on the Solid Rock of the Word of God and you must understand the Word correctly because it is the only thing that will help you to stand in the battle. Heaven and earth will pass away, but God's word will not pass away. It is settled forever in heaven.

It was necessary for Christ to win this personal victory over Satan before He could win a representative victory for all believers, because to be an atoning sacrifice, to pay the penalty for our sin, He Himself had to be without sin.

> When the devil had ended all the temptation, he departed from him for a season. And Jesus returned in the power of the Spirit. Luke 4:13, 14

Christ's power during His earthly ministry over sin, sickness, death, and demonic forces was founded upon this three-fold victory over temptation. Having overcome in the realm of the body, soul, and spirit, He returned in the power and the authority of the Spirit. Everywhere He went demons cried out and fled; the sick were healed; blind eyes were opened; the deaf heard; the mute began to talk; the cripple walked; the dead were raised; He multiplied the food and fed the multitude; He walked on the water; because of who He was and because of the victory that He had purchased in the wilderness.

This personal victory would not be enough for His perfect life to be available for you and me; there must be a Calvary. For the victory of Christ over demonic spirits we have to go back to His substitutionary death. First His life had to be totally victorious. Having qualified in that arena, He could now be a substitute for us and pay the penalty for our sin and give us victory over death. The victory of the Cross is now in our behalf.

> [Christ through Calvary blotted] out the handwriting of ordinances that was against us, which was contrary to us, and took it out of the way, nailing it to his cross; and having spoiled principalities and powers, he made a show of them openly, triumphing over them in it. Col. 2:14-15

> Now is the judgment of this world: now shall the prince of this world be cast out. John 12:31

> Of judgment, because the prince of the world is judged. John 16:11

More was happening on Calvary than just a cleansing for our sin. When Jesus died and rose again, He conquered Satan in at least five realms:

1. *He conquered Satan as the author of sin.* "The Son of God was manifested, that he might destroy the works of the devil" (1

John 3:8). Those works that brought sin into mankind were to be destroyed at Calvary. The work of Satan caused man to be alienated from God in what seemed to be an impossible situation, but:

> God was in Christ, reconciling the world unto himself, not imputing their trespasses unto them; and hath committed unto us the word of reconciliation. Now then we are ambassadors for Christ, as though God did beseech you by us: we pray you in Christ's stead, be ye reconciled to God. For he hath made him to be sin for us, who knew no sin; that we might be made the righteousness of God in him. 2 Cor. 5:19-21.

2. *He conquered Satan as the author of sickness.* One of the first fruits of sin is sickness. The reason man is susceptible to sickness is due to the fall. He has a body that is condemned to death because of sin. Because of Calvary the Christian has a resurrection body as his inheritance.

> Surely he hath borne our griefs, and carried our sorrows; yet we did esteem him stricken, smitten of God, and afflicted. Isa. 53:4

> When the even was come, they brought unto him many that were possessed with devils; and he cast out the spirits with his word, and healed all that were sick: That it might be fulfilled which was spoken by Isaiah the prophet, saying, Himself took our infirmities, and bore our sicknesses. Matt. 8:16, 17

> What? Know ye not that your body is the temple of the Holy Ghost which is in you, which ye have of God, and ye are not your own? For ye are bought with a price: therefore glorify God in your body, and in your spirit, which are God's. 1 Cor. 6:19, 20

Divine healing is as thoroughly reported in the Scripture as the forgiveness of sin, and any time that you try to justify the erasure of divine healing, you will, in order to be intellectually honest, have to erase the forgiveness of sin. To not preach the healing power of the Lord Jesus Christ along with the forgiveness of sin is to preach another gospel than what is written in the Word. Christ's victory on Calvary was for our bodies as well as our souls and our spirits, and there is healing for you at Calvary.

3. *He conquered Satan as the author of death.* Death came because of Satan's fall. Death means separation from God spiritually (in physical death our soul and spirit are separated from our body), but Christ came to bring the victory.

> I will put my trust in him. And again, Behold I and the children which God had given me. Forasmuch then as the children are partakers of flesh and blood, he also himself likewise took part of the same; that through death he might destroy him that had the power of death, that is the devil; And deliver them who through fear of death were all their lifetime subject to bondage. Heb. 2:13, 14

JESUS THROUGH CALVARY, DESTROYED HIM WHO HAD THE POWER OF DEATH. That means that as a Christian, Satan cannot take your life unless you are outside of God's covering because you have stepped into sin and are in a place of disobedience against God. Christ has authority over death, and you belong to Him.

> I am he that liveth, and was dead; and, behold, I am alive for evermore, Amen; and have the keys of hell and of death. Rev. 1:18

4. *He conquered Satan as a ruler of the kingdoms of this world.*

> And the seventh angel sounded, and there were great voices in heaven, saying, The kingdoms of this world are become the kingdoms of our Lord, and of his Christ; and he shall reign for ever and ever. Rev. 11:15

Jesus is going to take possession. We've had the wrong kind of tenant around here, Jesus has taken the title deed and He's kicking him out; the eviction notice is already given!

5. *He conquered Satan in the realm of the heavenlies,* over principalities and powers, in heaven and on earth.

> Wherefore he saith, When he ascended up on high, he led captivity captive, and gave gifts unto men. (Now that he ascended, what is it but that he also descended first into the lower parts of the earth? He that descended is the same also that ascended up far above all heavens, that he might fill all things.) Eph. 4:8-10

Wherefore God also hath highly exalted him, and given him a name which is above every name: That at the name of Jesus every knee should bow, of things in heaven, and things in earth, and things under the earth; And that every tongue should confess that Jesus Christ is Lord, to the glory of God the Father. Phil. 2:9-11

And what is the exceeding greatness of his power to us-ward who believe, according to the working of his mighty power, Which he wrought in Christ, when he raised him from the dead, and set him at his own right hand in the heavenly places, Far above all principality, and power, and might, and dominion, and every name that is named, not only in this world, but also in that which is to come: And hath put all things under his feet, and gave him to be the head over all things to the church, Which is his body, the fulness of him that filleth all in all. Eph. 1:19-23

Before the fall, we learn scripturally that those who died went into a place called Hades, often mistranslated as Hell. In Hades you had a place for the righteous dead and a place for the unrighteous dead. There was a gulf between, as we learn from the parable that Jesus told about the rich man and Lazarus. At Calvary, Christ spoke to the thief "You will this day be with me in Paradise." When He died, Jesus went down into Hades and one of the things He did was to preach the gospel to those spirits who had been captive there prior to the time of the patriarchs, and He took the departed righteous with Him into the heavenlies as He ascended to the Father. The place of righteous dead today is no longer in Hades but in a place now called Paradise in the third heaven.

There is a Scripture that says that "I will not suffer the Holy One to see corruption," or to stay in hell. When Jesus went down into Hades, He experienced death like you and I as Christians will never ever experience. He tasted death for us and made a way for us to overcome.

As Jesus went down into the depths of Hades, Satan and his emissaries were reveling. Satan, all through the history of mankind, had tried to destroy the Messiah. As we have seen, when Satan saw that the Messiah was going to come through the loins of Adam and Eve, he thought it would be through Abel because he was the one who was serving God, so Satan stimulated Cain to kill his brother. Then there were those who were corrupted by demonic influences, which resulted in the flood.

After that there was an attack on Noah and it went right on down to Abraham, Isaac, and Jacob; to the progenitor of Christ who should have been Reuben, the firstborn, but because of his sin was given unto others through the tribe of the Lion of Judah. A bastard was born of this tribe which would be a progenitor of Christ and for four generations would not be allowed under the law of Israel into the sanctuary. As a result, for four generations there was no specific persecution because Satan did not know who the Messiah would come through.

But then came King David with whom God made a covenant that his seed would rule forever and which would enlarge the Abrahamic covenant, bringing forth the Christ child. The household of David has been persecuted by the hatred of Satan ever since, culminating in our day with the tremendous holocaust of the Jews in Germany. We find that this same hatred came when King Herod heard the Christ child was born and ordered every boy three years of age and under in that region slaughtered. Satan tried to destroy the Messiah, thinking that if the incarnation of God in a human body was destroyed, it would forever be destroyed and he himself would become god of the universe.

But our Father would not allow His Holy One to see corruption, and when He died, Satan thought he had gained the eternal victory and was reveling in that deep, dark throne room of hell. Christ came into that room and marched right up to Satan, his knees began to wobble in fear, and he called on all the hosts of hell to hold back the Christ. But Christ just shook them off and marched right up to Satan, took out of his hands the keys of death, hell, and the grave, turned around and ascended up out of hell. As He did, He took His heel and smashed it into Satan's face, fulfilling the prophecy that says of the Messiah that Satan would bruise His heel but He would bruise the serpent's head, and He arose victorious to set us free forever more!

When He arose again, He brought forth victory in at least these five realms: He conquered Satan as the author of sin: He conquered Satan as the author of sickness; He conquered Satan as the author of death; He conquered Satan as the ruler of the kingdoms of this world; He conquered Satan in the realm of the heavenlies over the principalities and the powers in heaven and in earth; and the victory of Christ on the Cross has made Jesus Lord over all.

Who is gone into heaven, and is on the right hand of God: angels and authorities and powers being made subject unto him. 1 Peter 3:22

He is the King of kings, the Lord of lords; He is Lord over all! When you go to war, you need to know where your victory is. Christ had not only gained the victory over Satan in His life, but He gained the victory in His substitutionary death; not only so, but He also gained the victory over Satan in His resurrection and ascension. This includes Christ's victory in heaven.

Luke speaks of the seventy being sent out to heal the sick and to preach the gospel. As they came back they said that even the demons were subject to them through Jesus' name. And He said to them, "I beheld Satan as lightning fall from heaven."

> Behold, I give unto you power to tread on serpents and scorpions, and over all the power of the enemy: and nothing shall by any means hurt you. Luke 10:19

He has given us authority over *ALL* the authority of the enemy! He talked about it when He saw people being healed and the gospel being preached, and He said that what was happening in the spirit world was Satan falling as lightning from heaven. *Christian living which does not touch that realm falls short of the gospel description of Christianity.* You are not only called to be sons or mature children of God, but you are called to be soldiers of Jesus Christ who overthrow Satan's strongholds in the spirit world.

> And the great dragon was cast out, that old serpent, called the Devil, and Satan, which deceiveth the whole world: he was cast out into the earth, and his angels were cast out with him. And I heard a loud voice saying in heaven, Now is come salvation, and strength, and the kingdom of our God, and the power of his Christ: for the accuser of our brethren is cast down, which accused them before our God day and night. Rev. 12:9, 10

When did we see the salvation of Christ, the strength and the kingdom of God, and the power of His Christ? When Satan and his angels were cast out of the heavenlies into the earth. The only commentary on that in the Bible is when the seventy ordained of Christ went out, preached the gospel, and prayed for the sick. This Scripture speaks of the miracle ministry on earth in the demonstration of the victory of Christ that sets the captive free to lay hold of the liberty for which He gave His life on Calvary to purchase for mankind. There is at least a vital relationship between the enemy being cast out of the heavenlies and the delivering power of God going forth evangelistically on earth. That is warfare.

And they overcame him by the blood of the Lamb, and by the word of their testimony; and they loved not their lives unto the death. Therefore rejoice, ye heavens, and ye that dwell in them. Woe to the inhabiters of the earth and of the sea! for the devil is come down unto you, having great wrath, because he knoweth that he hath but a short time. Rev. 12:11-12

This is pictured as the culmination of the church age. God has been raising the church up and developing her for a purpose, not just to be His showcase but to bring forth the full expression of redemption on earth.

The believer can rejoice in Christ's full and complete victory over Satan's entire kingdom of darkness. All are conquered; all are defeated; all are subject to Christ. God has given Christ to be head over all things to the church and He must reign until all enemies are put under His feet.

For he must reign, till he hath put all enemies under his feet. The last enemy that shall be destroyed is death. 1 Cor. 15:25, 26

You and I may be some of the ones to taste this victory! This is the victory of Christ at the Rapture when the Christian has total victory over death, and the reason you have that victory is because there is no sin imputed to you. The wages of sin is death. There were those who had it by faith and never had it experientially because the fullness of time did not come. However, we are living in the generation the Scripture has marked out as the fullness of time and there are those here who most likely will be alive at the physical return of Jesus Christ for His church. They will so fully conquer death, having so fully conquered sin in their lives through the grace of Christ and His full work at Calvary, that death will no longer have a claim on them. One of the greatest acts of faith they will ever have is when they step out of this deathly body into one of immortality at the sounding of the trumpet known as the Rapture of the church!! People think the Rapture is just going to be some little escape hatch, but it is going to be an act of *faith.*

The blind eye opens, the crippled leg gets straightened; someone who never walked begins to get up and walk; cancer disappears; the deaf mute begins to hear and speak; someone with a terminal illness is healed; someone who has been dead for several hours is raised to life; faith grows; and the day comes when the trumpet sounds and you say, "Here I am, Lord." You conquer death, the last enemy. What Christ did on Calvary was for God and His church, and that is the kind of victory we have when we go to war.

Don't ever let the devil lie to you and tell you that you are defeated and in bondage; that you have to do what the devil wants you to do. You don't have to deal with him, because you deal directly with God and if you are fully submitted to God and are being obedient to Him and are knowledgeable of the things of God and allow Him to change you, you will find a progressive victory over the kingdom of darkness. With that progressive victory, you will also become a mature son or daughter of God. And as you become mature, you will discover that God wants you to be a soldier in the Spirit, to take His message of release and reconciliation to those who are yet held captive.

Father, thank You for the great victory You made available for us at Calvary. Help your people to understand the basis of victory, the wonderful weapons You have provided, and the objectives of spiritual warfare. Give your people purpose in battle so that they can accomplish something in their walk with You as soldiers of Jesus Christ. Help each one to understand that they can be effective as they hear the call of the Spirit to spiritual warfare so that the Church of Jesus Christ can go on to maturity and so that this world can be evangelized before the coming of our Lord and King.

6

The Ministry of the Church

> To make all men see what is the fellowship of the mystery, which from the beginning of the world hath been hid in God, who created all things by Jesus Christ: To the intent that now unto the principalities and powers in heavenly places might be known by the church the manifold wisdom of God. Eph. 3:9, 10

With what are we wrestling? With principalities and powers, not with flesh and blood. The gospel of Jesus Christ has this purpose among others: that the church, the Body of Christ, might make known to the principalities and powers the manifold wisdom of God. How?

The enemy in his rebellion was envious and jealous of the designed purpose that God had in creating man and wanted to interrupt that purpose. He wanted to be what God had designed man to be. He wanted the place in God's kingdom and creation that was created for man to occupy, a place of such depth and communion with God that man would be like God. Our destiny is to be conformed to the image of His Son. So there was jealousy, envy, and rebellion and Satan thought he gained a victory, but God, through Christ, overthrew the rebellion of Lucifer in his efforts with mankind as a *total and complete* victory for every Christian.

God has chosen the church to manifest that victory among mankind and thereby, by entering into the spirit world, overthrow principalities (regions) ruled by demonic spirits and powers (authorities) which are ruling in areas such as education, finance, and entertainment. Man, when he was created, was put on earth to have dominion. The dominion was lost in the fall and now Christ, as our Kinsman Redeemer, has purchased the legal right for the redemption of the planet Earth. He alone is worthy to open up the title deed of the earth (Rev. 5:5).

There are three areas in which Christ has delegated His authority to the church.

1. *Authority over demons and disease*

> He called his twelve disciples together, and gave them power and authority over all devils, and to cure diseases. And he sent them to preach the kingdom of God, and to heal the sick. Luke 9:1, 2

(Sent for a purpose: to preach the Kingdom of God and to heal the sick.)

> Behold, I give unto you power to tread on serpents and scorpions, and over all the power of the enemy: and nothing shall by any means hurt you. Luke 10:19

2. *He delegates authority to the church corporately*

> But ye shall not be so: but he that is greatest among you, let him be as the younger; and he that is chief, as he that doth serve. For whether is greater, he that sitteth at meat, or he that serveth? is not he that sitteth at meat? but I am among you as he that serveth. Ye are they which have continued with me in my temptations. And I appoint unto you a kingdom, as my Father hath appointed unto me; That ye may eat and drink at my table in my kingdom, and sit on thrones judging the twelve tribes of Israel. Luke 22:26-30

3. *Authority given to believers individually.* Here there is a qualification, their faith, as they believe.

> And he said unto them, Go ye into all the world, and preach the gospel to every creature. He that believeth and is baptized shall be saved; but he that believeth not shall be damned. And these signs shall follow them that believe. Mark 16:15-17

Are you a believer? If you are, where are your credentials? How do I know that you are a genuine believer?

> In my name shall they cast out devils; they shall speak with new tongues; They shall take up serpents; and if they drink any deadly thing, it shall not hurt them; they shall lay hands on the sick, and they shall recover. Mark 16:17, 18

> So then after the Lord had spoken unto them, he was received up into heaven, and sat on the right hand of God. And they [the believers] went forth and preached everywhere, the Lord working with them, and confirming the word with signs following. Mark 16:19, 20

If we are going to be involved in spiritual warfare, we must note that in each of these cases Christ gave authority related to proclaiming the gospel, healing the sick, and overthrowing ruling spheres of demonic spirits. When He gave the great commission, Jesus said that these signs would follow them who believe: they will speak with new tongues, they will lay hands on the sick and they shall recover, they will cast out demons. We find the effectiveness in warfare should be the credentials of a believer! Anyone who claims to preach the full counsel of God *must* be involved in proclaiming the Word, healing the sick, and overthrowing demonic spheres of influence. To proclaim the gospel of the Kingdom is to preach the Word, heal the sick, and cast out devils. Anything less is something different than the gospel of Jesus Christ.

The Lord is commissioning the church, which is His body. He did it with the twelve, he did it with the seventy, and he did it for everyone when He said these signs will follow those who believe. The commission of the church is to continue His ministry on earth, for this truly is the ministry of the Lord Jesus Christ.

The Book of Acts is the only behavioral interpretation of the teaching of Jesus Christ in the gospel; there is no other real commentary on what it is. So Acts demonstrates the power of this gospel on the basis of Christ's complete victory over all the power of the enemy. In Acts we see people baptized in the Holy Spirit; we see people healed; we see the dead raised; we see principalities and powers overthrown; we see magistrates dealt with by the supernatural intervention of God, causing people thrown in jail like Peter to be supernaturally brought out of jail; and we understand what Jesus was talking about. In Acts 26:18, Paul proclaims something of his calling as a preacher:

> To open their eyes, and to turn them from darkness to light, and from the power of Satan unto God, that they may receive forgiveness of sins, and inheritance among them which are sanctified by faith. Acts 26:18

Any activity of a Christian in spiritual warfare must have these purposes as their goal, or they are outside the authority of Jesus Christ. The authority is given to us to accomplish a goal, and that is to open the eyes of those who are blinded to the truth, to turn them from darkness to light, and to turn them from the power of Satan unto God. That is the intent which God has for the church, to make manifest the manifold wisdom of God unto the principalities and powers.

> These words spake Jesus, and lifted up his eyes to heaven, and said, Father, the hour is come; glorify thy Son, that thy

Son also may glorify thee: As thou hast given him authority over all flesh, that he should give eternal life to as many as thou hast given him. John 17:1, 2

Jesus' authority was for a purpose: to grant eternal life to as many as would come to Him. How is it manifested? If this is the ministry of Jesus carried on by the church, then we continue to go back to the life of Christ to see our example. In Matthew 12, Jesus healed a man who had been demonized, blind, deaf and dumb for forty years, and when He did so they accused Him of doing this by the power of the devil, and Jesus said in verse 28, "But if I cast out devils by the Spirit of God, then the kingdom of God is come unto you."

Bringing the Kingdom of God is something that is important. When Christ came into this world for His ministry, He had a forerunner—the greatest prophet of the Old Testament, according to Jesus—whose name was John the Baptist. John had a very simple message: "Behold, the kingdom of heaven is at hand. Repent, prepare ye the way for the coming of the Lord!" When Jesus began His public ministry, He preached the same message, and you and I have this same message. But when Jesus spoke it, He wasn't speaking of something ethereal, for He *was* the kingdom of heaven and as He came into our midst, the Kingdom of God and of life was there to set as many free as would repent. There was total and complete authority over all the power of the enemy to set a person free whose heart had turned towards God! If we preach that the Kingdom of God is at hand, it means that there is an authority of God at hand, an authority to set free and to deliver from the power of darkness. That is what spiritual warfare is all about.

One of the things that is wrong with many Christian efforts to evangelize is that they try to *explain* the gospel. God never asked you to go and explain the gospel to anyone as such; He asked you to preach it, to proclaim the truth. You are not to try to convince anyone that the gospel is true; that is the job of the Holy Spirit. The. Holy Spirit came to convince the world of sin and of righteousness and judgment. You try to do the job of the Holy Spirit and you are out of order—remember who you are! You are called to proclaim the truth, and when you proclaim it you can stand in the authority of Jesus Christ. The Spirit of God is backing up the truth and those who turn will experience the authority of God to deliver them from the influence of the enemy in their lives.

The believer has a relationship to the kingdom of darkness. First of all, the believer should not be afraid of that kingdom. One time I was in Edmonton, Canada, at a breakfast with three hundred people, sharing my testimony. As I did, a demon began to act up in a girl there and she began to scream and writhe around on the floor. Many of those people had never seem a demon act up. Often it is one of the best things that can happen to a church because it makes them aware that this isn't a philosophy, this is reality. I ministered deliverance to that girl, she was set free, and received the Lord Jesus. I had their attention then! But many of those people sitting there who saw that demonic manifestation were afraid. The devil always works in an atmosphere of fear. Fear paralyzes faith and releases unbelief. God always works in an atmosphere of love, and the Scripture says that faith works by love (Gal. 5:6).

For God hath not given us the spirit of fear; but of power, and of love, and of a sound mind. 2 Tim. 1:7

Secondly, the believer should not be ignorant of Satan's devices. You should avail yourself of the spiritual armour and weapons provided by Christ's victory.

Lest Satan should get an advantage of us: for we are not ignorant of his devices. 2 Cor. 2:11

Ignorance provides an opportunity for Satan to get an advantage over you. When you are in war, *he who hesitates gives the advantage to the enemy.*

Anything that goes down in history about Richard Nixon will contain a positive note about his involvement in foreign relations. He is probably one of the most brilliant foreign relations people in our century. He understood foreign affairs: he really understood the Soviet mentality; he really understood what was happening on a global basis and the role of the United States of America. He made some statements that were quite interesting. The Russian mentality is one that has been built upon knowing bitterness and war after war. They are used to it, they are ready for it, they are hardened for it, and they are ready to act. War is nothing new to them and they will go to war if they think it will help them gain their end. The American mentality is no war, last resort, peace at any cost; no matter how much we compromise our freedom, let's not go to war. Nixon says such a mentality is a very dangerous thing as far as international balance is concerned because if we hesitate in certain situations, it will give enough advantage to the enemy to win.

That is true in the natural, and it is also true in the spiritual. When we are ignorant of the enemy's devices, when we put positive regard to the heart of Satan and give him just a little bit and don't have a killer's instinct in our spiritual warfare, we hesitate and give the advantage to the enemy and he wins the battle. One of the devices of Satan is to lull us into a place where we hesitate, where we ignore. The Scripture tells us that such a thing gives the enemy the advantage.

(For the weapons of our warfare are not carnal, but mighty through God to the pulling down of strong holds:) Casting down imaginations, and every high thing that exalteth itself against the knowledge of God, and bringing into captivity every thought to the obedience of Christ. 2 Cor. 10:4, 5

The weapons of our warfare are not carnal. One of the things we are to do is to see everything that exalts itself against the knowledge of God and every thought brought into the captivity and obedience to Christ. We are to open the eyes of the blind, to turn people from darkness to light, from the power of Satan to God, that they might receive the forgiveness of sins and the inheritance of faith. When we do so, we find that the enemy blinds the hearts of those who believe not lest the light of the gospel should shine into them and they be converted (2 Cor. 4:4). Our weapons work in the realm of the mind to bring down reasonings, knowledge, imaginations, fantasies, rationalizations, anything that exalts itself against the knowledge of God and to bring them into captivity and obedience to Christ.

What happens when you watch television? What is television designed to do? To cause you to identify with some of the characters. In doing this, you imagine yourself to a degree carrying out the role of that character in the story. And a story that you can't "relate" to is one that you can't identify with. The enemy uses this purpose to develop a mentality, a knowledge, a thought process, a response pattern to life that is antichrist. That doesn't mean you cannot watch TV without having that happen, but you must be selective about what you watch.

Slowly but surely, the mentality of our country is being changed and molded through these kinds of things, and the enemy knows what he is doing. Warfare has to do with overthrowing the influences of demonic spirits and a fallen sin nature in our daily life.

EXPERIENCING THE FULL VICTORY OF CHRIST IS KNOWN AS WE RECOGNIZE OUR COMPLETE IDENTIFICATION WITH HIM. There must be an identity change, which Paul speaks of in Romans 7. He says that he notices a different law in himself. There is a law in his mind that agrees with the law of God, and there is a law in his body that is contrary to the law of God, doing or desiring to do the things that he believes he shouldn't do. He would rebel against the things he knew he should do; therefore, he said, "It is no longer I doing them, but the sin nature that dwells in me."

All of your life you have lived with an identification of yourself developed in your fallen nature, with its aspirations, its desires and response patterns, and you have your self-image in Adam. *But victory in warfare begins by first of all finding our identification in Christ:*

1. THE BELIEVER'S POSITION LEGALLY.
a. *We are in Christ and are partakers of the divine nature.*

Blessed be the God and Father of our Lord Jesus Christ, who hath blessed us with all spiritual blessings in heavenly places in Christ: According as he hath chosen us in him before the foundation of the world that we should be holy and without blame before him in love; Having predestinated us unto the adoption of children by Jesus Christ to himself, according to the good pleasure of his will, To the praise of the glory of his grace, wherein he hath made us accepted in the beloved. In whom we have redemption through his blood, the forgiveness of sins, according to the riches of his grace. Eph. 1:3-7

Whereby are given unto us exceeding great and precious promises: that by these ye might be partakers of the divine nature. 2 Peter 1:4

Having come into Christ, we have many exceedingly precious promises given to us that through them and the exercise of faith, we might be partkers of the divine nature. We are to live in that nature, we are to live by His life. This is accomplished by a process of appropriating the promises of God and growing in our relationship with Him.

b. *We are new creatures.*

If any man be in Christ, he is a new creature: old things are passed away; behold all things are become new. 2 Cor. 5:17

If you are a new creation, you are no longer the person who existed before Christ. When I give my testimony, I find it very

69

interesting that my self-concept is not at all identified with the person I was before I was saved; that person was someone else who died in January, 1968. I am a new man with new attitudes, new motivations, new values, a new spirit, and new abilities. If you are a Christian, you are a new creation. For your identity to change, you must begin to identify with who you are in Christ.

c. *We are in the kingdom of the Son.*

Who hath delivered us from the power of darkness, and hath translated us into the kingdom of his dear Son. In whom we have redemption through his blood, even the forgiveness of sins. Col. 1:13, 14

We have been translated out of the kingdom of darkness; it is no longer our residence. We are now residents of the kingdom of God's dear Son and we are seated in heavenly places with Christ.

d. *We are seated in heavenly places.*

Wherein in time past ye walked according to the course of this world, according to the prince of the power of the air, the spirit that now worketh in the children of disobedience: Among whom also we all had our conversation in times past in the lusts of our flesh, fulfilling the desires of the flesh and of the mind; and were by nature the children of wrath, even as others. But God, who is rich in mercy, for his great love wherewith he loved us, Even when we were dead in sins, hath quickened us together with Christ, (by grace ye are saved;) And hath raised us up together, and made us sit together in heavenly places in Christ Jesus: That in the ages to come he might shew the exceeding riches of his grace in his kindness toward us through Christ Jesus. For by grace are ye saved through faith; and that not of yourselves: it is the gift of God. Eph. 2:2-8

Therefore, *we have a heavenly position,* and in spiritual warfare you must operate from that position. If you operate from any other, you will fail to gain the victory. You must stand in your heavenly position, like "king on the mountain", when you get on top of the mountain, you must plant your feet and stand.

Put on the whole armour of God, that ye may be able to stand against the wiles of the devil. Eph. 6:11

Take unto you the whole armour of God, that ye may be able to withstand in the evil day, and having done all, to stand. Eph. 6:13

In order to stand, you must plant your feet on something solid, immovable in war, and you have to hold your ground against the onslaught of the enemy. Such is your legal position as a Christian: you are in Christ. The enemy will come to you and say you are not in Christ, that you are not a partaker of the divine nature. He will question your motives and accuse you of many things. However, you must stand and say, NO, I AM IN CHRIST AND I AM A PARTAKER OF THE DIVINE NATURE! WHAT I WAS BEFORE DIED AT CALVARY AND I'M A NEW CREATION IN CHRIST! I'M SEATED IN HEAVENLY PLACES AND I'M LOOKING DOWN ON THE CIRCUM-STANCE; I'M STANDING IN THE PLACE OF VICTORY. I'VE BEEN DELIVERED FROM THE POWER OF DARK-NESS, I'M A RESIDENT OF THE KINGDOM OF THE SON AND I'M STANDING IN THAT POSITION! You must recognize this confession as truth and reality and stand in that place. If you let go of one of these positions, it will cause you to stumble in the battle.

2. THE BELIEVER'S RESPONSIBILITY EXPERIEN-TIALLY

a. *We must live victoriously over the sins of the flesh,* thereby giving Satan no ground on which to stand against us, so that he has no handle in us. How do you give the enemy a handle? By sins of the flesh, such as maintaining a wrong attitude towards one who slighted you in the past, or justifying a lack of discipline or disobedience.

Hereafter I will not talk much with you: for the prince of this world cometh and hath nothing in me. John 14:30

Jesus said that Satan would come to inspect His humanity but he would find no handle in Him. God sometimes allows the enemy to come and inspect you. First John says to love not the world, neither the things in the world because they are of the world and not of the Father. If you have a love of the world, the things of the world, the worldly lifestyle, or the kingdom of darkness, or if there is still that favorite little sin that you like to hide somewhere and actually there's a little love for it in your heart, then you have given the enemy a handle in your life. When the enemy comes along and inspects your life and finds a handle in you, he uses it to overthrow you. *The only people who can really be effective in spiritual warfare are those who at the moment of battle are in a place of full surrender to Jesus Christ.* Their relationships are right with God and with their fellow man. If not, they won't stand in the battle.

"Neither give place to the devil" (Eph. 4:27). How do you give place to the devil? By sins of the flesh that you haven't overcome, wrong attitudes, or the love of the world. Galatians 5:19-21 lists adultery, fornication, idolatry, witchcraft, schools of opinion, spirit of competition, dissention, sedition, and drunkenness as expressions of the sins of the flesh.

    b. The believer must *keep himself in the love of God* so the enemy will not be able to touch him.

> Herein is our love made perfect, that we may have boldness in the day of judgment: because as he is, so are we in the world. There is no fear in love; but perfect love casteth out fear: because fear hath torment. He that feareth is not made perfect in love. 1 John 4:17, 18

> We know that whosoever is born of God sinneth not; but he that is begotten of God keepeth himself and that wicked one toucheth him not. 1 John 5:18

My first pastor was devastated by a phrase in a book she was reading that said, "You love Jesus about as much as the one whom you love the least." "In that you have done it to the least of these, my brethren, you have done it unto me." There are times when loving is difficult. People may be intruding upon an activity that is very important to us, and to love them means we have to drop that activity for them. Sometimes when we don't succeed we end up with resentment and fall out of the love of God. We must guard our spirits to be sure we are in the love of God.

    c. The believer must submit to God and *then* resist the devil.

> Submit yourselves therefore to God. Resist the devil, and he will flee from you. James 4:7

Notice the order. Many people having problems with demonic attacks come for counseling. When you tell them they don't have to be subject to these demons and tell them of their authority in Christ and teach them how to take authority over it, some don't gain any real victory. Normally it is because they haven't forgiven someone and have bitterness and resentment; there is something that God asked of them and they withheld it; or there is something God is wanting them to do and they refuse to do it. *There is a lack of submission to God.* The only person who can have authority in Christ is the one who is *under the authority of Christ.* In the measure that you are under Christ's authority, to that degree will you have His authority.

3. THE BELIEVER'S BATTLEGROUND

Satan attacks in three areas of our being: body, soul and spirit.

a. *Spirit.* The spiritual part of our being is the area where our intuition functions, our conscience (approving/disapproving) functions, and is the place where we commune with God. It is that part of you which knows what you are thinking and which observes your thought patterns (1 Cor. 2:11).

But he that is joined unto the Lord is one spirit. 1 Cor. 6:17

The Spirit itself beareth witness with our spirit, that we are the children of God. Rom. 8:16

If you are a genuine Christian, born again, then your spirit is joined to the Spirit of God and you are one Spirit. If God is joined to your spirit, and you are one Spirit with Him, then there is no way that you can become demon possessed unless you have a falling out with God and He no longer dwells in your spirit. If your spirit is one with God's spirit, and you say you are demon possessed, then you are saying that God is under the control of a demon spirit and you are confused about who is Lord! The word "possession" means to be under the control (not influence) of another, and if your spirit is one with God's, then you cannot be under the control of a demon spirit. If a person is controlled by a demon spirit, he is not saved. The enemy attacks the believer's spirit to confuse, condemn and mislead.

b. *The soul—the real battleground in spiritual warfare.*

I beseech you therefore, brethren, by the mercies of God, that ye present your bodies a living sacrifice, holy, acceptable unto God, which is your reasonable service. And be not conformed to this world: but be ye transformed by the renewing of your mind, that ye may prove what is that good, and acceptable, and perfect, will of God. Rom. 12:1, 2

The soul is the realm of your mind, will, and emotions. The Scripture tells us that we are transformed by the renewing of our mind. We are not to be conformed to the lifestyle of this world, but be metamorphasized by the renewing of our mind that we might be able to prove, or demonstrate, live in, walk in, manifest what is that good and acceptable and perfect will of God. Even though you are born again, you are not able to manifest the acceptable will of God until you are transformed by the renewing of your mind.

Every thought has an emotional value to it. The thought that trickles through your mind triggers an emotional response. Fighting for our will is the enemy and God, because the the essence of sin and defeat is to bring our will into a choice against the authority of God. So Satan works on our mind, our emotions, our spirit and our body in order to overthrow our will. When the enemy tries to overthrow you, he is going to target your will. The bottom line will be: do you choose to obey God or do you not? He will fill your mind with all kinds of rationalizations and excuses and it is amazing what Christians will allow themselves to believe. I have known some who become involved in adultery and have pages and reams of rationalization and say it is all right for them before God. They are full of demonic lies that have overthrown the will. "I just couldn't help it. This desire was just raging within me." What is the Lord of your life? Jesus Christ or your feelings? Who are you serving? Are your feelings serving you or are you serving them? *If you serve your feelings and allow them to dictate your choices,* THEN YOUR FEELINGS HAVE BECOME YOUR GOD.

Why art thou cast down, O my soul? and why art thou disquieted in me? hope thou in God: for I shall yet praise him for the help of his countenance. Ps. 42:5

Bless the Lord, O my soul: and all that is within me, bless his holy name. Ps. 103:1

David's feelings were trying to get the best of him, but we see him taking authority over his feelings and commanding his soul to bless the Lord. You may say, "I don't feel like it." What does that have to do with it? God says to bless the Lord, and that means you have to take authority over your feelings as you do a rebellious child and bring them into submission.

Your feelings aren't to rule you, and the enemy is going to try to aggravate the wrong feelings to get at your will. That is where his fiery darts work, and they come with an oppression or a depression, a stimulation of fear or unbelief, lust, evil thoughts, emotional and mental torment, or accusation. One time this really became alive to me. I was going to the University of California in undergraduate work and often studied between classes in order to get mileage out of my day. I was sitting in a lounge reading and doing my homework when all of a sudden, my whole body was tingling with stimulation. I lifted my head, looked behind me and saw a young girl walking by with a heavy spirit of lust. I was engrossed in study when that spirit attacked and began to emulate. This is the enemy's purpose, to distract the will from the Spirit of God.

Others say, "I'm depressed today." The fruit of the Spirit is love, joy, peace, and longsuffering. Surrender your life to God and obey Him, for the fruit of righteousness is peace. "If I only felt like it, I'd obey God." If you obey God, *THEN* you will feel like it.

We are to recognize these fiery darts from the enemy and they are to be quenched by spiritual weapons.

> For though we walk in the flesh, we do not war after the flesh: (For the weapons of our warfare are not carnal, but mighty through God to the pulling down of strong holds;) Casting down imaginations, and every high thing that exalteth itself against the knowledge of God, and bringing into captivity every thought to the obedience of Christ. 2 Cor. 10:3-5

The Korean War was fought in Korea, the Vietnamese War was fought in Vietnam, the Christian warfare is fought in the battleground of the mind, and our weapons are not carnal but spiritual.

> For out of the heart proceed evil thoughts, murders, adulteries, fornications, thefts, false witnesses, blasphemies: These are the things which defile a man. Matt. 15:19, 20

> For as he thinketh in his heart, so is he: Eat and drink, saith he to thee; but his heart is not with thee. Prov. 23:7

There are three sources of thought and there are three kinds of spirit in the world. All thought is born out of spirit and comes from the spirit of man, the Spirit of God or the spirit of antichrist. If it is the spirit of man, be sure it is sanctified or reject it. If it is a spirit of antichrist, deal with it by the power of the Spirit and the Word of God. If it is the Spirit of God, receive it.

> When Jesus came into the coasts of Caesarea Philippi, he asked his disciples, saying, Whom do men say that I the Son of man am? And they said, Some say that thou art John the Baptist: some, Elias; and others, Jeremiah, or one of the prophets. Matt. 16:13, 14

That was man's thought.

He said to them, But whom say ye that I am? And Simon Peter answered and said, Thou art the Christ, the Son of the living God. And Jesus answered and said unto him, Blessed are thou, Simon Bar-jona: for flesh and blood hath not revealed it unto thee, but my Father which is in heaven. Matt. 16:15-17

That was God's thought.

From that time forth began Jesus to show unto his disciples how that he must go unto Jerusalem, and suffer many things of the elders and chief priests and scribes, and be killed, and be raised again the third day. Then Peter took him, and began to rebuke him, saying, Be it far from thee, Lord; this shall not be unto thee. But he turned, and said unto Peter, Get thee behind me, Satan: thou art an offense unto me: for thou savourest not the things that be of God, but those that be of men. Matt. 16:21-23

A demonic spirit had put that thought into Peter's mind.

As a Christian you can control your own thoughts (from your own spirit) at will. For example, think of what you had for lunch today. Think of the last time you took a bath or a shower. Think of what your mother looks like. You can do it; you can choose what you think about and you can take your mind and control it by willpower. Now, if thoughts are coming through your mind and you *can't* control them when you earnestly try to, that shows you they are not from your spirit, because you cannot control the thoughts of another person by willpower. Another person can tell me his thoughts, but I cannot control his thoughts by my will because he is another being. If thoughts are coming through my mind and I cannot control them, it is because they are from another being and if they are the wrong kind of thoughts, they are demonic. There is only one way to get authority over demonic thoughts and that is through the power and authority of the Lord Jesus Christ to take dominion over them and to demand them to go. You don't have to be subject to a gutter thought life.

    c. *The body.* The third area where the enemy attacks is in the body, the temple of God, the area of the five senses. The enemy attacks us with illness, disease, and infirmities. He also attacks us in the appetites and instincts that God gave man and tries to stimulate us to an inordinate expression of the five basic drives of man: self-preservation, acquisition, hunger, reproduction, and dominance.

4. THE BELIEVER'S ARMOUR

Here is an outline of the believer's armour, to be looked at in detail later.

a. *The Word of God*

Ye shall know the truth, and the truth shall make you free. They answered him, We be of Abraham's seed, and were never in bondage to any man: how sayest thou, Ye shall be made free? Jesus answered them, Verily, verily, I say unto you, Whosoever committeth sin is the servant of sin. John 8:32-34

One piece of armour is the word of God. If you are serving sin and yielding to it, you need to know the truth. In spiritual warfare we are called upon to open the eyes of the blind and turn from darkness to light. We need to know the Word of God because *if we are ignorant of the truth, we are susceptible to the enemy.* There are many things which we do in our lives that are not according to God's will because we are ignorant. Every one of you as Christians, as you grow in the knowledge of God and His will as you have grown in your walk with Him, have discovered things in your life that have been there for months and sometimes years which you thought were all right but in fact were contrary to God's will. When you understand truth in such an area of your life and made an appropriate adjustment, a whole area of difficulty became an area of blessing.

You shall know the truth and the truth shall make you free. When you have a need, sympathy is not going to help you. You do need empathy: you need someone to cry when you cry and rejoice when you rejoice, but you don't need sympathy. You need *truth.* If you take the truth and thank the Lord, if you embrace the truth, it will set you free. When you go to war, the only thing that you can stand on is the truth of the Word of God. If you are just wondering about a truth and don't really know it, then you won't be able to stand in confidence.

b. *The Name of Jesus*

Whatsoever ye shall ask in my name, that will I do that the Father may be glorified in the Son. If ye shall ask anything in my name, I will do it. If ye love me, keep my commandments. John 14:13-15

Wherefore God also hath highly exalted him, and given him a name which is above every name: That at the name of Jesus every knee should bow, of things in heaven, and things in earth, and things under the earth; And that every tongue should confess that Jesus Christ is Lord, to the glory of God the Father. Phil. 2:9-11

Another armour piece is the use of the name of Jesus. There is power and authority in the name of Jesus. The phrase "in the name of Jesus" tacked onto the end of a prayer like a rubber stamp is not what is talked of here. There is nothing wrong with acknowledging that you are praying in the Lord, but saying "in Jesus' name" has no magical power. *It is a phrase that speaks of praying or acting in union with the will, with the motivation and with the intent of the heart of God.* When your intent, will, and motivation are in harmony and in union with the heart of God's will, intent and motivation in your action or word, then you are in the name of Jesus. The phrase "in my name" speaks of a life union. If you read the context here you will find that everything Jesus talked about was how He and the Father were one, and we would be one with Him as He was one with the Father. Then He says, "Whatsoever you ask in my name."

c. *Christ in you*

For whatsoever is born of God overcometh the world: and this is the victory that overcometh the world, even our faith. Who is he that overcometh the world, but he that believeth that Jesus is the Son of God? 1 John 5:4, 5

Greater is he that is in you, than he that is in the world. 1 John 4:4

Christ in you is a weapon of your warfare. You must learn to abide in Him, to act out of Him and not out of yourself.

d. *The Blood of Jesus*

[Christ] Whom God hath set forth to be a propitiation through faith in his blood to declare his righteousness for the remission of sins that are past through the forebearance of God. Rom. 3:25

The blood of Jesus Christ is another piece of armour that we have. We have righteousness because of the cleansing of the blood of Christ—the blood covenant.

e. *The Power of the Holy Spirit*

But if I cast out devils by the Spirit of God, then the kingdom of God is come unto you. Matt. 12:28

For to one is given by the Spirit the word of wisdom; to another the word of knowledge by the same Spirit: To another faith by the same Spirit; to another the gifts of healings by the same Spirit; To another the working of miracles; to another prophecy; to another discerning of spirits; to another divers kinds of tongues; to another the interpretation of tongues. 1 Cor. 12:8-10

The gifts of the Spirit are weapons for our use in warfare. We need the power of the Spirit of God in our life. How does that come? Jesus said that after the Holy Spirit is come upon you, you shall receive power, or divine enablement, and you shall be His witnesses in Jerusalem, Samaria, Judea, and the uttermost parts of the earth. Witnesses of the power and reality of the resurrected Christ. How? Through the operation of the gifts of the Spirit.

There is a concept which some have that "I have this gift of the Spirit and I have that gift of the Spirit. I have the gift of the word of knowledge; or I have the gift of prophecy; or I have the gift of healing." I don't *have* any gifts. I have the Baptism of the Holy Spirit and I have the person of the Holy Spirit who manifests Himself in the various ways described here in 1 Corinthians 12. I have seen every one of those described gifts manifested in my life on various occasions where they were needed to accomplish a purpose in God. When you have the power of the Spirit of God dwelling in you and you are a yielded vessel, He will manifest the gift of the Spirit which is needed at any particular time.

Christ will manifest Himself to you in many ways. The meaning of the Hebrew phrase, "I am" literally is "I am ___ ," that is, *"I am whatever you need me to be."* That is the way God is! He is the same yesterday, today, and forever, and when the life of Christ is dwelling in you, He will be to you what you need Him to be in your circumstance.

f. *The Whole Armour of God*

Finally, my brethren, be strong in the Lord, and in the power of his might. Put on the whole armour of God, that ye may be able to stand against the wiles of the devil. For we wrestle not against flesh and blood, but against principalities, against powers, against the rulers of the darkness of this world, against spiritual wickedness in high places. Wherefore take unto you the whole armour of God, that ye may be able to withstand in the evil day, and having done all, to stand. Stand therefore, having your loins girt about with truth, and having on the breastplate of righteousness; And your feet shod with the preparation of the gospel of peace; Above all, taking the shield of faith, wherewith ye shall be able to quench all the fiery darts of the wicked. And take the helmet of salvation, and the sword of the Spirit, which is the word of God: Praying always with all prayer and supplication in the Spirit, and watching thereunto with all perseverance and supplication for all saints. Eph. 6:10-18

Notice that the only offensive equipment for the armour of God listed here is the sword of the Spirit. Every other piece of equipment is protective. Notice there is nothing on the backside, 79 so if you turn tail and run you will be in trouble! All of the defensive equipment is on the front for a forward onslaught and the only offensive piece of equipment mentioned is the sword of the Spirit, the Word of God, the *rhema* of God.

g. *Praise*

I have discovered another offensive weapon in the Scripture— it is called praise.

> Let the high praises of God be in their mouth, and a two-edged sword in their hand; To execute vengeance upon the heathen, and punishments upon the people; To bind their kings with chains, and their nobles with fetters of iron; To execute upon them the judgment written: this honor have all the saint. Ps. 149:6-9

> Sing aloud unto God our strength: make a joyful noise unto the God of Jacob. Take a psalm, and bring hither the timbrel, the pleasant harp with the psaltery. Blow up the trumpet in the new moon, in the time appointed. Ps. 81:1-3

This 81st Psalm speaks of a feast period and is saying, "Let's get out and rejoice and have a praise festival!" However, the people refused to do it. This is what could have happened if they had obeyed:

> Oh that my people had hearkened unto me, and Israel had walked in my ways! I should soon have subdued their enemies, and turned my hand against their adversaries. The haters of the Lord should have submitted themselves unto him: but their time should have endured forever. He should have fed them also with the finest of the wheat: and with honey out of the rock should I have satisfied thee. Ps. 81:13-

People get upset when they walk into a church where people are worshiping and praising the Lord; they think they are fanatics. It is all right for people to go to a football game and become absolutely wild. I don't know if that's as worth getting excited about as the salvation of our Lord Jesus Christ, but the enemy always fights genuine worship that is in spirit and truth, and if he can't shut it off he will try to pervert it by fleshly manifestation and to stimulate worship that is not from the heart. Genuine worship that is in spirit and truth is a mighty offensive weapon against the enemy to overthrow his strongholds and to cause him to be submitted and defeated by the power of Almighty God. Don't ever apologize for genuine worship; we need more of it! The next time you hear opposition to it, recognize its source.

> Whoso offereth praise glorifieth me and to him that ordereth his conversation aright will I show the salvation of God. Ps.50:23

There is a beautiful Hebrew translation of this verse: *"Whoso offers praise glorifies me and I will open up a way before him that I might show forth my victory!"*

So we have outlined seven areas of Christian armour. We must have the Word of God; we must learn to walk in the understanding of the use of the name of Jesus; we must recognize Christ in you is greater than he that is in the world; the place of the blood of Jesus Christ and the blood covenant; the power of the Holy Spirit; the whole armour of God in Ephesians 6; and the place of praise and worship. If we are serving God as He intends, we are called to be more than sons and people who get victory over sin in our lives. God has called us to be soldiers; He has sent us to be effective warriors for the Kingdom of God, to overthrow the demonic powers ruling in principalities and high places, in order that the eyes of the blind might be opened, that they might be turned from darkness to light, from satanic power to God, and that they might receive forgiveness of sin. God has chosen the church, you and me, as His instruments to accomplish this in the world. If we won't, then our generation goes by the wayside because God has laid the privilege and responsibility on our shoulders.

Father, thank You for your Word, thank You for making a full provision for us. You have given us a position in your kingdom. You have privileged us to carry a responsibility with You in the great commission. You have shown us the battlefield and equipped us with spiritual weapons and armour. Help us to assess our spiritual responsibilities as soldiers. Cause us to be trained and prepared that we might war a good warfare for Jesus' sake. Amen.

7

Flowing With the Spirit

We have taken a look at the authority given to the church, and now we need to see how that authority is exercised. This will include looking at the vast importance of recognizing the wiles of the devil and how to deal with them. The main focus here is the volition of man and the spirit of God working in man. This is an area which is very unique in spiritual experience from that which you find outside of the Kingdom of God. As a result, there are many people who are under misconceptions, who do not understand what it means to respond to or yield to the Spirit of God and therefore are bound by ineffectiveness.

Principle: THE HOLY SPIRIT WORKS THROUGH OUR LIVES ONLY WITH THE ACTIVE COOPERATION OF THE WILL OF THE BELIEVER. When you walk with God in a mature relationship, you like to see Him use you on purpose and with design, not by accident. God is gracious to intervene once in a while in spite of us, but He is not obligated to intervene in this way. He does so at times because of His loving kindness. However, if we are going to work with God in assurance and walk with Him in an effective ministry with design, where we see things accomplished, we must understand this very important principle: The Holy Spirit works through your mind, your will and emotions (the soul), and through your body *only* with the active cooperation of the believer's will.

> Whereunto I also labor, striving according to his working, which worketh in me mightily. Col. 1:29

Notice Paul's cooperation with the Spirit. *I* labor according to the working of the Lord or of the Spirit of God who is working in me, which works in me mightily. Jesus said it in John 5:17: "My Father worketh hitherto, and I work." We can see in Christ the principle that is involved, for Jesus said, "I do nothing but what I see my Father do" (John 5:19). He had a spiritual perception. He did not act out of His own initiative, but His will was actively engaged in harmony and cooperation with the manifest will of God. He only spoke as God gave Him the word to speak. He said,

> For I have not spoken of myself; but the Father which sent me, he gave me a commandment, what I should say, and what I should speak.

It did not come out of His own mind or initiation.

Believers often have a concept that we are to be just like a hose and the Spirit of God is to be like water flowing through the hose and all we do is yield. This has hindered many people from moving with the Spirit of God. God *always* invites and requires the active participation of the believer. If you were in any other spiritual walk, you would find that you would not be actively involved, that all of your activity would have a design to bring you to a place of passivity. If African witch doctors needed a spirit to come upon them in order to perform whatever they wanted to do, whether walking across red hot coals or sticking things through their lips, they would drink and swing their heads around and dance in a frenzy until they came to a point where they had passivity of mind and will. At that point the spirit would come upon the witch doctor. Yoga, Buddhist meditation, etc., have as a goal to bring you to nothingness, death if you would, a total passivity of mind and will.

God is different. An example is Moses leading the people of Israel out of Egypt. They came to the Red Sea followed by Pharaoh and his army, and the people started crying to Moses that he brought them there to be destroyed. Moses prayed and asked God to do something and God said, "Moses, why are you standing here praying?" *Do* something: Stretch forth your rod" (Ex. 14:15, 16). As he did a wind came up and blew through the night and opened the Red Sea so they could cross over on dry ground. What had happened? There was a supernatural manifestation of God in relationship to an active participation of His servant. Moses exercised his will in unity with the will of God and there was a release of God's power.

EVERY SUPERNATURAL ACT OF GOD RECORDED IN THE SCRIPTURE THROUGH A HUMAN VESSEL IS PRECEDED BY AN ACT OF THE HUMAN WILL. We see then an opposite: the patterns of the satanic kingdom, and the Kingdom of God. God governs the believer as Lord by the believer's co-acting will. God wants you to actively use your will to participate in what He is doing. In the satanic kingdom the enemy wants you to passively yield.

Reigning In Life

[As we have received the] abundance of grace and of the gift of righteousness, [so we] shall reign in life by one Jesus Christ. Rom. 5:17

Man, by the power of the Holy Spirit with his will under the lordship of Christ and energized by the Spirit of God, is to rule himself first of all. You cannot effectively go to war if you do not rule yourself.

He that hath no rule over his own spirit is like a city that is broken down, and without walls. Prov. 25:28

Understand the context of this Scripture in the day in which it was written. It was a time where the arsenal for warfare was horses, slingshots, and bows and arrows. A place of security would have strong walls around it or be set on top of a hill. They did not have airplanes, missiles, or a means of slinging weapons over high walls, nor did they have guns and dynamite. So a place of security would have a strong wall, and he that does not rule his own spirit is likened unto a city whose walls are broken down. What are you going to do if you go to war and your walls are broken down? You will be defenseless and what will happen to you? Even though Christ has given you authority over the power of the enemy, you will not be effective in war if you do not rule over your own spirit.

The spirits of the prophets are subject to the prophets. 1 Cor. 14:32

Sometimes we say, "Oh, I couldn't help myself," such as when someone bursts out in tongues for a message to be interpreted or a prohecy at a time when it is not in divine order. There is an order to the operation of the gifts of the Spirit. As soon as you confess that you couldn't help it (if your confession is true), you have confessed it was not the Spirit of God because the spirit of the prophet is subject to the prophet. We are to rule over our own spirit, it is to be under our control and we have a stewardship responsibility before Jesus Christ to rule our spirit.

We are also to rule in the realm of our mind and emotions.

Finally, brethren, whatsoever things are true, or honest, or just, or pure, or lovely, of a good report, if there be any virtue, if there be any praise, think on these things. Phil. 4:8

Our thought life is to come under our control.

Set your affection [or your mind] on things above, not on things on the earth. Col. 3:2

We are to set our thoughts and affections within certain boundaries as described in God's Word. We are to take authority over our own mind and emotions. All of your life you have been taught by the world that you are to be true to what you feel—be true to your heart. If you are going to be true to your heart you will go straight to hell! The heart of man is desperately wicked; who can know it? (Jer. 17:9) That means you will have to control and deal with your fallen nature. There is no good thing in the natural man; it is the life of God in you by the miracle of the new birth through salvation which is good and it is that life flow of God that must be released. Therefore, you must control your thought life and your feelings and your volitional life in order to see the Spirit of God manifested. You cannot have the luxury of carrying vengeance, unforgiveness, resentment, or bitterness in your heart. You do not have the privilege as a born-again Christian, redeemed by the Blood of the Lamb, bought with a price, not belonging to yourself, to luxuriate in thoughts about when someone hurt you and relive that situation in your mind over and over again. It is sin and forbidden of God and you are responsible to deal with it, to forgive and seek reconciliation with the individual. Take the injury to God and let Him heal it and set your thoughts, attention, and affection on the things that God has given in His Word.

If you do not control your thought life, you won't be any good in war because as soon as you go to battle, the enemy will start sending some fiery darts that will land in your mind and manifest themselves as thoughts such as, "Do you remember what that person did to you," or "God can't use you."

Sometimes the enemy comes along and stimulates our emotions, but WE are to rule! We aren't to just say, "Oh well, here it comes. Let's just let it flow." Put on your Holy Ghost filter to get rid of all the wrong thoughts, attitudes, and feelings as you rule in your spirit and your soul.

You are also to rule in your body.

If any man speak in an unknown tongue let it be by two, or at the most by three, and that by course; and let one interpret. But if there be no interpreter, let him keep silence in the church; and let him speak to himself, and God. 1 Cor. 14:27, 28

You must control what you are doing with your body, and this passage deals with our tongue and speech. We *can* control what we do with our body. What did James say about the tongue? A very wicked member, hard to control, but if we don't rule and control our bodies and go to war, what happens? Our speech can set the course of nature on fire of hell.

Even so the tongue is a little member, and boasteth great things. Behold, how great a matter a little fire kindleth! And the tongue is a fire, a world of iniquity; so is the tongue among our members, that it defileth the whole body, and setteth on fire the course of nature; and it is set on fire of hell. James 3:5-6

Jesus said you will be justified by your words, and you will be condemned by your words (Matt. 12:37). As a Christian you will give an account for every idle word that you speak (Matt. 12:36). Your words either release life or release death; as it says in Proverbs, the power of life and of death is in the tongue (Prov. 18:21).

We can control what we do with our body, and if we don't rule by the Spirit, exercising our willpower to rule in our spirit mind, emotions, and body, then we will be ineffective in war.

WHAT IS WILLPOWER?

The more common word for it is character. Your character is revealed by the choices you make in every-day life. Character is also made or destroyed by the choices you make. When we talk about being made into the likeness and image of Christ, we are talking about His character. The *character* of Christ is to be built into us, which means as we are confronted with choices, the choices we make are the ones that Christ makes. The things that we filter out and the things we allow to come in are as Christ would filter out or allow to come in.

You cannot make the right choices in yourself. There is no way that you can have an effective warfare against the enemy's world or really control your thought life as you want to without being a Christian because thoughts come from either God, man, or the devil, and if they come from the spirit of antichrist, you cannot control them without the authority of Christ.

All of our ruling is dependent upon John 1:12: "As many as received him, to them gave he power to become the sons of God." The phrase "sons of God" speaks of mature relationship with the Lord; not just a child of God but sonship in terms of having been adopted into maturity. Once saved, you are not immediately governed by the Spirit, you are not spiritual all at once. You still have a lot of flesh that gets in the way. What is dealt with is your will. In the midst of your trial and in the midst of the dealings of the Spirit of God and the providential workings of God in your life, in the midst of an exhortation, in the midst of your prayer and in the message of God brought to you in one form or another, *there is always one focus, and that focus is your will.* What are you going to do with it? An obvious example is the message of salvation. You can hear it a hundred thousand times but when you respond there is only one thing that counts at all, and that is the choice you make: to act upon the gospel message and receive salvation or to say no, and there is no in-between.

Incidentally, every time you try to put off surrendering to the Lord, you are in the midst of rebellion because the Scripture says, "The times of this ignorance God winked at, but now he commands all men everywhere to repent." God has commanded you to repent of your sin and delay is an expression of direct rebellion against the commandment of God. If the truth of God comes to us in any way, it requires a change in our life and there is a commandment that comes with it: repent or obey. When that commandment comes, it is focused on our will. Our will is to turn away from something and turn into something. It is not enough to come out, you also have to come in. It wasn't enough for Israel to come out of Egypt, they had to come into the Promised Land. That is part of what repentance is all about and that is what every dealing of God is about. Our will is involved and we must choose to cooperate and will with God!

> The night is far spent, the day is at hand: let us therefore cast off the works of darkness, and let us put on the armour of light. Rom. 13:12

This is something you must do; it is an act of the will. If you do not act by your will in this regard, the works of darkness will remain in your life and the armour of light will not be present. Jesus has broken the dominating power of darkness and sin and has made a full provision in Himself for the armour of light and the victory of Christ. In order for you to be free from darkness and to possess that light, you must exercise your will to put off darkness and to put on light!

It gets right down to choice: What are you going to do with it? Spiritualize it all you want, cry about it all you want, excuse it all you want, give me a hundred thousand reasons why it is difficult, give me a million reasons why you don't understand, it doesn't matter. When you get down to the bottom line, WHAT ARE YOU GOING TO DO WITH YOUR CHOICE? You receive it and put on light and put off darkness, or you reject it. "Well, I don't feel like it." So what? If you want to get your feelings straightened out, then what you need to do is put your will in harmony with the will of God. If you don't feel like it, that is a good testimony that you have been acting wrong! "I don't feel like worshiping the Lord. I don't feel like praying. I don't feel like going to church. I don't feel like reading the Bible." You know what you are telling me? "I've been living in sin. I've been saying no to God." That's the truth, and truth is the only thing that sets you free from deception.

> Put off concerning the former conversation, the old man, which is corrupt according to the deceitful lies. Eph. 4:22

> Put on the new man, which after God is created in righteousness and true holiness. Eph. 4:24

> Lie not one to another, seeing that ye have put off the old man with his deeds; And have put on the new man, which is renewed in knowledge after the image of him that created him. Col. 3:9, 10

Mortify therefore your members which are upon the earth: fornication, uncleanness, inordinate affection. Col. 3:5

Neither yield ye your members as instruments of unrighteousness unto sin; but yield yourselves to God, as those that are alive from the dead and your members as instruments of righteousness to God. Rom. 6:13

In whom also ye are circumcised with the circumcision made without hands, in putting off the body of the sins of the flesh by the circumcision of Christ. Col. 2:11

Put ye on the Lord Jesus Christ, and make not provision for the flesh, to fulfill the lusts thereof. Rom. 13:14

These are just sample passages of hundreds in the Scripture which describe a decisive act of the will towards things that are unseen. So many times we think our willpower is related to things seen: you choose to get in the car or not; you choose to eat a hamburger or chicken. Those are all things in the natural, but notice all of these Scriptures are related to things that are unseen, the spiritual, and they show the effects of man's will acting in harmony with the liberating power of Christ. When you set your will with the will of God, it releases the power of Christ to set you free. We have learned that the pattern of Satan's temptation is to et at your will, your volition, to choose for him as opposed to choosing for ·God. The most fundamental expression of this pattern was when God told man not to eat of the Tree of the Knowledge of Good and Evil for on the day he did it, he would die, and Satan said he would not surely die. *The choice you make has eternal consequences.*

Christ did everything necessary to provide all that we must have for total and complete victory in our lives when He gave His life on Calvary and rose again the third day. But in order to move out of the realm of provision in the abstract and into the realm of subjective experience where it is manifested and applied in our lives, we must engage the action of the will in cooperation with the Spirit of God. That is fundamental if we are going to war because the will is the area which the enemy will attack and it is the area in which you must be obedient to God, and as you are obedient to Him in your will, the victory is sure. If you stumble in the area of the will, the enemy gets a victory in the battle and if he wins too many battles, he wins the war!

We must understand this fundamental: when you go to war, know what the enemy is after. The enemy wants you to get distracted; he is after your choices. When you go to war, the first things to check are your choices, your will, and your options. Are you choosing with God?

> Wherefore, my beloved, as ye have always obeyed not as in my presence only, but now much more in my absence, work out your own salvation with fear and trembling. For it is God which worketh in you both to will and to do of his good pleasure. Do all things without murmurings and disputings. Phil. 2:12-14

The Spirit of God is working in us to make us willing and to enable us to do His good will. Christianity is only a problem when you don't have the "want to." When you know that you ought to but don't have the "want to," and you know that the source of battle is over the will, then you can go to the Lord and ask Him to give you the "want to." GOD WILL GIVE YOU DIVINE MOTIVATION. HE WILL MOTIVATE YOU FROM WITHIN BY PLACING DESIRE IN YOUR HEART THAT WAS NOT PREVIOUSLY THERE. If you have a desire for the things of the Lord in any way, shape, or form, that desire is an example of what the Scripture is talking about.

It says in Romans 3 that there is none righteous, there is none that seek after God. Your natural man will *not* seek after God. The seeking after God with a genuine sincerity of heart, with a sincere desire to know Him in reality, is born of the Spirit of God; it is the fruit of God's working in you to will and to do of His good pleasure.

In that hour of regeneration, when we are born again, God gives man the decisive liberty of will to rule over himself as he walks in fellowship with God. When you became a Christian, God liberated you from the dominating power of sin. Romans 6 says your sin nature will no longer have dominion over you. You might allow it to manifest, but you are able to rule that nature and to rule that sin! This also holds true with the enemy that has worked in your life for years. When you became a Christian, his power was broken off of your life and Christ gave you power and authority over all the power of the enemy. YOU HAVE IT! The problem is not the provision; *the problem is your willingness to use it.*

A person was calling me who was concerned about her spouse, telling me how her spouse was going through this trial and how he really wanted God. He wanted to know about the Baptism of the Holy Spirit and came in for counseling. One of our evening services was dedicated to helping people get baptized in the Holy

Spirit. This man took the afternoon to discuss the baptism but wouldn't even come into the service; he turned right around and went home. This went on for a couple of months, a crisis came and "now he's *really* seeking God." I started asking questions. Has your husband been baptized in the Holy Spirit yet? No. Is he really seeking after it? No. Please don't tell me he is really seeking after God when you have something as fundamental as the Baptism of the Holy Spirit. He knows the truth about it. It has been shown to him in the Word. He knows it is biblical and says he wants it, but he won't seek after it. What you are saying and what he is doing are two different things. God does not want lip service; he wants *action* from the will.

If we are going to follow God, we must make a choice, and by the restoration of a free will to act in choosing for God, Satan loses his power. *It is at the point that our will is liberated and we put it in harmony with the will of God,* actively deciding to choose and to do the will of God, *that the power of Satan is broken in that area of our lives.* He leaves with fear and trembling. Christians, because of wrong concepts of yielding to the Spirit of God, have had a passivity of will instead of exercising their will.

Satan is spoken of in the Scripture as the god of this world, and he rules the world through the will of men who are enslaved by him. He does it directly by enslaving people, and indirectly by making them enslave each other by causing them to cover the power of influence or control over others. Obvious examples are Stalin, Hitler, Lenin, etc.

In time past ye walked according to the course of this world, according to the prince of the power of the air, the spirit that now worketh in the children of disobedience: Among whom also we all had our conversation in times past in the lusts of our flesh, fulfilling the desires of the flesh and of the mind; and were by nature the children of wrath, even as others. Eph. 2:2, 3

If you go to war to see someone liberated, you must get to the will. What holds that will? The lusts of the flesh, the desires of the mind, wrong concepts, and blindness hold the will in bondage. Second Corinthians 4:4 says that the god of this world has blinded the minds of those who believe not lest the light of the gospel should shine into their hearts and they should be converted.

A woman came to see me who was demon possessed whose problem was sex. She was raised in a Pentecostal church, knew the Bible says to not be unequally yoked with unbelievers yet married a non-Christian at the age of 19. She got divorced and married again around 24. Again she divorced and married again around 30, and divorced. All marriage were with unbelievers. Everything she told me about her life related to how she chose against the will of God. I asked her to tell me about her Christian experience. She went to church and taught in Sunday school, but she was always getting hung up because they told her not to do this or not to do that. Never once was there any conversation about meeting the Lord or communing with Him. I told her she wasn't saved and had never been born again. She said she had been to the altar, cried, and asked Jesus to forgive her sin, but I told her it was not enough. You cannot have Jesus as Saviour if you don't have Him as Lord. You want Him to be your Saviour and you want His blessing and deliverance, but you won't let Him be Lord of your life. You choose over and over again to go against the will of God and now you're hung up with a demon. I told her if she wanted to be free, she had to give herself up to the lordship of Jesus Christ. "I don't know if I could ever be celibate." "I don't know if the Lord has asked you to be celibate, but if He did you must be willing and trust Him to meet your needs." She needed *truth*. There was no deliverance from those demons working in her life without the lordship of Jesus Christ. Her choice for Him was the key to deliverance.

It comes right down to a choice. Are you going to let Jesus Christ be Lord or not? All of us have gone the way of this world, according to the prince of the power of the air, fulfilling the desires of the flesh and of the mind, and we know what the fruit of that is. If you choose the will of God, you have a different kind of fruit: love, joy, peace, longsuffering, gentleness, meekness, temperance, faith.

Man must *deliberately* place his will on God's side. When you go to war, you must be in a place where you are abiding in God's will. Remember that warfare has a goal. The authority we have in Christ is related to taking dominion over the powers of darkness holding people in bondage so they can come out of the kingdom of darkness and into the kingdom of light, from Satan to God, that they might be set free and be partakers of the inheritance that is in Christ. *Our goal in warfare is to liberate people so they choose the will of God.*

The action of the will is governed by the understanding of the mind. David was running from God and said, "If I descend down even into hell, lo, thou art there." Once truth comes to you by the illumination of the Holy Spirit, you can run to the depths of hell and you cannot get away from it. That is why it is important that you give others the truth, regardless of how they respond. Has truth ever come to you and you didn't want it? It's like a goad. You use goads to get stubborn bulls moving, and the Scripture says the Word of God is like a goad to us.

I remember the first time I encountered truth. I went out and wanted to get stoned. I tried but it didn't work—I couldn't enjoy it anymore! Truth came and I saw sin for what it was, at least in a measure, and it lost it's pleasure.

The Word says in Romans 1 that when the people continued to turn away from God, he turned them over to a reprobate mind, a dead mind that is unable to respond to truth. Many people, because they don't want truth, would rather be dead than to have to face it.

That is why they crucified the Christ. Truth comes and you have two reactions: you receive it, accept correction, and repent; or you justify yourself and try to get away from it—and you can't get away from it because it haunts you everywhere you go. When you can't get away from it and you don't want to receive it, there is only one choice left, and that is to try to put it out. So they crucified the Christ, but He rose again, because you cannot put out the Light who is God!

One of our offensive weapons is truth, the Word of God, the Sword of the Spirit, and the Holy Spirit uses truth. *The action of the will is governed by the understanding of the mind.* If you have a wrong understanding, then you continue in the results of that wrong understanding. Truth comes, you may not want to receive it, but the Holy Spirit bears witness to it and brings it back again and again to your mind.

I had a philosophy class at the University of California. I had A's all the way through my tests but I received a B because the professor didn't like my participation and discussion. The class would get way out there somewhere in discussion and find out that what they had was confusion. They didn't have anything that could resolve the dilemma they would come to. That is because there is only one absolute truth in any area and that is the person of Jesus Christ. So I didn't care which direction they went. I would sit and listen until they got into the dilemma and would raise my hand. Pretty soon they would try to avoid calling on me; they knew what I was going to say. I would present Jesus Christ, the truth, in the area they were discussing, whether it had to do with ethics or morals or knowledge, and it would resolve. They didn't want it to resolve, at least if it was with Christ!

Two TM'ers there would ask me how I could believe in that stuff. I would just share the gospel with them, and they would be irate with me. About a year and half later I was preaching a camp meeting in Calgary, and one of those TM'ers came up to me and told me she could never get away from what I said in that philosophy class. It haunted her, and about a year later she saw a tent meeting, went in, and got saved and filled with the Spirit. She was at that time going to Bible school in Calgary and was going to be a missionary in Taiwan.

So you want to give truth to people in warfare. When you do, it works on the will until finally you exercise the will either for or against God. When you exercise it for Him, the Spirit of God energizes that will and produces a result.

FINDING THE HOW TO'S

For I know that in me (that is, in my flesh) dwelleth no good thing: for to will is present with me; but how to perform that which is good I find not. Rom. 7:18

You have the "want to" but now you need the "how to." One reason why many churches are spiritual incubators for years is because the preaching from the pulpit does not get to the "how to's." Somewhere along the line we have to learn how.

In order to understand "how to's," we must begin to understand the difference between the soul and spirit. You are a tripartite being. You are made body, soul, and spirit. Your *body* is that part of you that is world conscious through your five senses: sight, smell, sound, taste, touch. Your *soul* is made up of your intellect, your volition and your emotions. It is the seat of your personality, the area of self-consciousness or self-awareness. Your *spirit* has a function not of a Freudian conscience but where the Spirit of God brings a conviction of approval or disapproval, an intuitive knowing; you only know in your spirit. You understand in your intellect, but the place where you commune with God is in your spirit. You find people all hung up in their intellectualisms who cannot commune with God because they are on a mind trip, they are in the soul. Others are on a feelings trip and cannot commune with God because they have to feel it all the time. There isn't anything wrong with feelings or intellect; they have their place, but that is not where you commune with God.

It is out of the spirit that everything which is genuine in God must find its beginning. I listened to a couple of different groups singing at a camp meeting recently. Some had spirit and some were soulish. Some would stir your emotions in a measure, get your mind going off on some kind of a thought, but it didn't get you to God. Others would minister their music and you would find your spirit leaping out towards the Lord, hungering for and responding to Him. One was in the Spirit of God, and one was soulish. It might have had all Christian words but it was soulish in its manifestation. That which is born of flesh is flesh, and that which is born of Spirit is Spirit.

For what man knoweth the things of a man, save the spirit of man which is in him? even so the things of God knowth no man, but the Spirit of God. 1 Cor. 2:11

What is that inside of you that knows your thoughts and feelings? There is a part of you that is watching what is passing on the view screen of your mind. That is your spirit, the part that knows the things of man.

The Spirit itself beareth witness with our spirit, that we are the children of God. Rom. 8:16

For if I pray in an unknown tongue, my spirit prayeth, but my understanding is unfruitful. 1 Cor. 14:14

That is what is good about tongues: you bypass the limitations of your concepts and of your intellect and you allow your spirit to have expression without those limitations. He says in verse 15 that he also prays with the understanding and with the Spirit.

What motivates your will? The will is central and vital because the choice of the will, whether it be for God or not, determines your destiny, determines the outcome, determines the victory or the defeat. God is a spirit, so God in the Spirit works in you to will and to do of His good pleasure. The motivator comes from the Spirit.

Your will is in a unique position. Because it is in the soul, it receives input from your body and from your spirit. The vehicle through which it receives input is the mind. Your mind gets all kinds of input from the natural world through the five senses, and through science we have various means by which we have enlarged the sensitivity of our senses. But it is still our five senses at work bringing to our mind input to affect our will.

A walk with God is not after a knowledge derived from the senses. If we walk by faith, we do not walk after the things that are seen. Notice the choices we had to make, to put off and put on things unseen: darkness and light, the deeds of the old man and the new man renewed in righteousness. We walk by faith and must focus our will through the mind and our understanding, the Spirit giving us input. That is illumination of the Word of life. For example, guidance—principles from the Word of life that teach us how to discern what is genuinely from the Spirit of God. If we can discern what is from the spirit, then we can take our will and place it there. We will be like Paul: if the will is present, how to perform we know not, but God teaches us. We learn guidance and then set our will in harmony with the will of God and come to victory. How does this work:

For the word of God is quick, and powerful, and sharper than any twoedged sword, piercing even to the dividing asunder of soul and spirit, and of the joints and marrow, and is a discerner of the thoughts and intents of the heart. Heb. 4:12

The Word of God applied like a sword cuts between soul and spirit, because the Word of God shows the desires and intents of the heart, and when the desires and intents of the heart are towards the will of God, embrace them. If not, put them off. You must exercise your will.

If you are going to be effective in war of any kind, you must learn to rule your own spirit, your own soul, and your own body; you must learn to deliberately exercise your will in the will of God; you must learn to discern the will of God and allow the Word of God to be applied to divide asunder between soul and spirit, the thoughts and intents of the heart. And then you must *by choice* not go with your gut-level feeling or with what you feel like doing, but you must actively and deliberately put off darkness and put on light, put off falsehood and put on truth, put off self and put on the Kingdom of God! Sometimes it will take everything that is in you, but the Scripture says when you have the willingness but you don't have the power to perform, it is God who works in you to will and to do of His good pleasure. It is in that hour that you call upon the Lord and say, "Thou mighty Christ, come forth in me!" When you pray that prayer, I want you to know that the resurrected Son of God can stand up inside you. The Person of the Lord Jesus Christ stands up strong because you set your will with the will of God and release Him to manifest His resurrected life through you. This is the way to victory.

Lord, I thank You for the reality of the authority we have as believers. I thank You, Lord, that as we have received You that You have given us divine enablement, the ability to become the mature sons of God, that sin will no longer have dominion over us, that the fallen nature is defeated, that the power of the enemy is under the power You have made available to us as Christians. Father, I recognize the importance of our choice, that we cannot have a passivity of will, that our will must be set in harmony deliberately with your will and as we do, we can call upon You to come forth in our Spirit and to manifest your resurrected life in our minds, wills, and emotions, to be released through our body and touch the world round about, to be released in the spirit world and cause the powers of darkness to bow, to set men and women free, to heal them in their bodies, to heal them in their minds, to heal them in their spirits, to heal them in their emotions that have been scarred by sin. Father, I thank You for the promise, that it is You that works in us to will and to do of your good pleasure. I pray, Lord, that You will work within us that motivating of your Holy Spirit in order that we might yield, actively, not passively yield, by understanding what the will of the Lord is through the Spirit of wisdom and revelation illuminating the Word of life, that we might deliberately set our will in harmony with your will. Lord, I believe You for it and thank You for it in Jesus' name, Amen.

8

The Battleground of the Mind

Every war has a battleground and the battleground in spiritual warfare is the mind. On that ground the victory will be won or lost.

For though we walk in the flesh, we do not war after the flesh: (For the weapons of our warfare are not carnal, but mighty through God to the pulling down of strong holds;) Casting down imaginations [or reasonings, or rationalizations], and every high thing that exalteth itself against the knowledge of God, and bringing into captivity every thought to the obedience of Christ. 2 Cor. 10:3-5

Notice the warfare is mighty through God to pull down strongholds, strongholds being defined as imaginations, reasonings, and everything that exalts itself against the knowledge of God, to bring into captivity every thought to the obedience of Christ. That means you cannot have a passive mind. You must exercise your will in order to use your "Holy Ghost filter" in your mind. There are thoughts that you reject and thoughts that you receive.

And having in a readiness to revenge all disobedience, when your obedience is fulfilled. 2 Cor. 10:6

When do you avenge disobedience in war? When *your* obedience is fulfilled. Don't get the order mixed up. If you come against a rebellious spirit, whether it comes in man or in the enemy, without having fulfilled your obedience, look out because the enemy is going to filet you. He has the killer's instinct and he won't quit when you are down.

All thoughts are born of spirit: the spirit of man, the Spirit of God, or the antichrist. If a thought comes from the Spirit of God, you should receive it. If it is born from the spirit of man, it can come from your fallen nature, so it must be controlled. The Bible says that as many that receive Him gave He ability to become the sons of God (John 1:12). That means you have the ability to control your thoughts by a simple exercise of choice. The Scripture tells us in James 4 to submit to God and then resist the devil and he will flee from you. The enemy can put thoughts in your mind and when that happens, you are not able to control those thoughts by your willpower—you must rely upon the authority of the name of Jesus Christ. Also, you cannot successfully come against the work of the enemy until you have submitted to God. If you cannot control the thought, then it is from the enemy, but you can take rule and dominion through the authority that is yours in Christ, *provided you have met the qualifier*: your obedience is fulfilled and you are submitted to God. To be submitted to God may mean that you should be correcting some relationship with your fellow man. For example, in the Sermon on the Mount, Jesus said that when you come to the altar to leave your gift and remember that your brother has ought against you, you are to leave your gift, go back to your brother and be reconciled, then return and offer your gift and it will be accepted. If you have something that is wrong in your attitude or behavior towards another and you have not corrected it, then you are vulnerable in war.

War is not for children. An outline of growth from one particular view can be seen as:

1st plane - Salvation
2nd plane - Baptism of Holy Spirit
3rd plane - Sonship, where we overcome our carnal nature
              and begin to consistently walk in the Spirit
4th plane - Warfare

Struggling with your flesh against the Spirit of God is not really the battle in genuine warfare. The enemy may intensify that battle, he may try to keep you from the knowledge of God or may try to keep you in carnality, but the war that we are talking about requires that we come into a degree of maturity to experience.

When we discover that all thoughts come from one of these three sources, then we know how we must deal with them.

And to make all men see what is the fellowship of the mystery, which from the beginning of the world hath been hid in God, who created all things by Jesus Christ: To the intent that now unto the principalities and powers in heavenly places might be known by the church the manifold wisdom of God. Eph. 3:9-10

Here we see that one purpose of the gospel is to make all men see the fellowship of the mystery (that is, our union of life with God), which from the beginning of the world has been hid in God who created all things by Jesus Christ, to the intent that *now* (not in the future) unto the principalities and powers in heavenly places might be known *by the church* the manifold wisdom of God. The Church of Jesus Christ, exercising its authority.

In light of the Book of Ephesians, we learn many things about war. There are three major areas that this book talks about:

1. The beginning of Ephesians deals with what we have in Christ as Christians. You have been blessed with all spiritual blessings in heavenly places in Christ; you were

made to sit together in heavenly places in Christ. You have this inheritance in Him, your wealth as a Christian.

2. The second section of Ephesians deals with our walk before the Lord, and that is where you deal with your relationship with others. For example, in Ephesians 4 we are exhorted to let no corrupt communication come out of our mouth but that which ministers grace to the hearers; he that stole, let him put away stealing; don't give place to the devil; be angry and sin not; put off the old man and put on the new.

3. The last chapter of Ephesians deals with warfare.

These *three areas* in the context of Ephesians point out three areas *where Satan will attempt to deal with the believer*. The first is to remove the Christian from his wealth. A second area where the enemy will attack is to lead the Christian astray from his walk before the Lord so that his relationship and practical expression of Christianity is awry. The third area is to disable the Christian from being a good soldier and fighting a good warfare.

THE CHRISTIAN'S WEALTH

The one army on planet earth that does not take care of its wounded is the Body of Christ. Many times there are those who have been wounded by the enemy and we have found ourselves drifting from them or letting the wounded go without embracing them and helping them to be restored. We are in a real war, we are soldiers in Jesus Christ, and one of the worst things that can happen to an army is to forsake its wounded. What happens to the loyalty? What happens to the unity? What happens to the strength of that army when the wounded are forsaken? We need to stand together, naturally and spiritually. We should always have an open heart to those who have been wounded. Christians have been wounded for various reasons, including poor leadership that has ended up leading them into the ditch. When the blind lead the blind they both go into destruction. When you have this kind of a problem, you may have sincere but unprepared, unqualified people, and it leads someone to a point where they are injured and unable to relate to leadership with confidence. They have wounds that need ministering to but they cannot open up to the ministry that heals the wounds. They are a casualty of war and one needs not to be condemnatory but understanding.

Leadership is a target of the enemy and sometimes fails, possibly because there was no one who really stood with them in the midst of the battle. They didn't have the confidence in a relationship with someone with whom they could open up and allow the battle to be seen, where they could be strengthened and ministered to. Why? Because some people think that the leaders in the Body of Christ are to be perfect. There are no perfect leaders, but because they are afraid to be transparent, because of the hypercriticism of those around them, because of fear of rejection and the resulting failure of their ministry, they try to hide it, hang in there and win it on their own, and they are sometimes overthrown.

I believe Jesus is calling the Church of Jesus Christ to a new dimension of war. It is part of the meaning of the Feast of Trumpets which has already been sounded for the church and it involves relationship, restoration of wounded individuals, a joining together and pressing on for righteousness and responsibility to one another. AN EFFECTIVE ARMY IS RELATIONSHIP ORIENTED. The Scripture says that one puts a thousand to flight and two put ten thousand to flight. It follows that three will put 100,000 to flight, etc.

Our inheritance in Christ is ours as we possess Him. He is our riches; the riches of God in Christ Jesus are ours as Christians, but participation in them is dependent on our being in a right relationship and position with Him. Because of the great abundant wealth and provision that God gives us in Christ, the enemy targets separating us. The expression of our inheritance is dependent upon right relationship and the enemy wants to break that relationship in order to dislodge us from our position in Christ which is far above all in heavenly places. In other words, the enemy tries to get you down in the dumps. You have to stay on top of the circumstances instead of under them. *We must fight from the position of king on the mountain.* WE HAVE THE VICTORY IN CHRIST, we don't have to GAIN the victory in Christ. Now we must MAINTAIN THAT VICTORY BY FAITH. Having done all to stand, stand that you might withstand in the evil hour. The enemy wants to target our position in Jesus Christ; he wants to take us out of that poistion so that we don't fight from the place of victory but fight from the place of trying to gain victory! Once you try to gain victory, you have already been overthrown.

COLDNESS OF HEART

The enemy would first try to wean the Christian away from Christ by coldness of heart. If he can develop a coldness of heart, he will draw us away from Christ and then he is prepared to weaken the believer's faith in Christ's Word through blindness of mind. Most of the difficulties which people are having intellectually are not really mind problems, they are heart problems because they don't have an ear to hear. Satan wants to draw your heart away from the Lord with something else. *He wants to rob you of your love for Christ and then of your loyalty to Him.* We see this in the letters to the Seven Churches in Revelation. "Nevertheless I have somewhat against thee because thou hast left thy first love." The excitement of our walk with God becomes cold and stale. We find that this church in Revelation which lost its first love was commended because it was loyal to the work of God and truth was waged in war against the lies of the devil with great intensity, but the *love for Christ Himself waned.* That is what I call becoming religious. They had all the right form, doing all the right things, but their heart throb towards the Lord was lost and distracted.

DOUBT

The enemy will seek to remove us from our position in Christ in several ways. One is *coming as an angel of light.* The real battle is not so bad when the enemy comes in his devil suit—his pitchfork, tail, and red suit. You don't receive him because you clearly recognize that he is the devil. But when he comes as an angel of light and you receive him thinking, "this might be the Lord," then he succeeds in overthrowing your position. Second Corinthians 11:13-15 speaks of this. *Through doubt he tries to dislodge you from your position in Christ which is held by faith.*

As long as we are here on earth we are going to be in the presence of doubt. I remember the first time I saw a genuine miracle of Christ. I knew the person, I knew the condition, and I knew intellectually that in order for them to be doing what they were doing, God had to have performed a miracle, but in my heart I said, I can't believe it. It didn't fit in my theology. I recognized that I had unbelief in my heart and as I grew in the Lord I came to the place where I had to deal with that unbelief. I began to realize that no matter what happened I had doubt. So I had to learn what to doubt. Do I doubt the Word of the Lord that God has spoken to my spirit and recorded in the written Word, or do I doubt my doubts of God's Word? I learned that instead of doubting God's Word which is reliable, I should doubt my doubts which were unreliable. I started to use my doubt in a correct fashion.

The enemy wants to confuse you regarding faith. That is what Satan did to Eve when he came into the garden and said, "Has God said that you shall not eat of this tree in the garden?" By bringing doubt to God's Word, he seeks to dislodge us from our place in Christ. "Has God said that we were all born sinners? Has God said that those who don't receive Christ shall suffer eternal damnation? Has God said that He will judge the sinner? How can such a God be a God of love?"

We learned that when Satan fell, the essence of sin was rebellion against God's authority. When God, who changes not and who cannot lie, declares something that has been confirmed with five immutables like this Word of God (the Bible) and has magnified that Word above all His name, then for you to doubt that Word is to be from an evil heart. Unbelief is spoken of as sin in the Scripture, because when we entertain doubt, we have entertained a rebellion against the integrity of God and His Word.

The enemy gives suggestion by question and when that thought comes through our minds, we think things like, "Maybe it's truth," or "I don't understand it, and if I don't understand it, it can't be real." There is a teaching that was going around not too long ago that said that the fall took God by surprise. That didn't happen because Christ was slain from before the foundations of the world as a provision for fallen man. God knew all about it, but these people could not accept the truth of God's Word because according to their own statements, "I can't conceive of a God who in His foreknowledge would allow man to fall, therefore it couldn't be." That means that "my mind is God and anything beyond my mind doesn't exist." It is a form of humanism and that is antichrist.

You don't know God by your intellectualism. The Scripture says that God in His wisdom ordained that man by wisdom would not know God (1 Cor. 1:21). You cannot know God by your mind; He is spiritually discerned. If you could know God through your mind, some of those who are not well endowed as others would be in bad shape!

DISOBEDIENCE

There is another way the enemy tries to get us dislodged from our position and that is through disobedience. Having established in Eve's heart doubt in God's Word, Satan then came out with a blatant denial: "You will not surely die." In this way he leads to disobedience. There are many false teachers in the church today who would lead one to disobedience to God, beginning by questioning God's Word, compromising it, and substituting it with something else. But God's Word has not changed.

When the enemy takes us out of our position in Christ, we cannot function effectively in warfare and our wealth in Christ is not experienced because through disobedience we have been dislodged from our ordained position. We are to be in readiness to have vengeance against all disobedience *when* our obedience has been fulfilled. When you have disobedience, you are not in a position in Christ to wield the Sword of the Spirit in aggressive warfare against the powers of darkness. You must be in right relationship or God will not back you up. That doesn't mean you have to be perfect, but when you stumble, put it under the Blood right away and if it involves someone else, reconcile that relationship. You don't play with it; you immediately cover that base.

DELUSION AND DECEPTION
The enemy tries to remove us through delusion and deception. There are many satanic cults today through which one may be led astray and new cults have been designed for our scientific generation, such as transactional analysis, EST, Lifespring, TM, Scientology and Moonies. Less obvious than the cults are things like secular humanism which has been slipping into the church. It has a concept that man was born innocent. "It's not my fault that I sinned. The reason that I'm like I am is because my parents were so hung up and because their parents were hung up. Everyone was hung up so it's not my fault, it's the mysterious 'they' who are at fault." The born innocent concept carries with it the idea that you can live a life of righteousness without God. That has been taught all over this country and it is delusion, capable of dislodging Christians from their position.

DEFLECTION
The enemy tries to remove us through deflection. A prime example of this is the Galatian church which began in the Spirit and attempted to grow in the flesh.

Have ye suffered so many things in vain? if it be yet in vain. He therefore that ministereth to you the Spirit, and worketh miracles among you, doeth he it by the works of the law, or by the hearing of faith? Gal. 3:4, 5

That which came by faith they wanted to do by works. That is deflection. In other words, if I touch not this and I eat not that, then I'm going to be spiritual. Becoming spiritual may involve some of those things but that is not the means by which one matures. The means to get there is faith and obedience towards God.

CONFUSION
Satan seeks to corrupt the mind from the simplicity of the gospel (2 Cor. 11:3) and to confuse the minds of earnest believers. He tries to bring confusion.

Now we beseech you, brethren, by the coming of our Lord Jesus Christ, and by our gathering together unto him, That ye be not soon shaken in mind, or be troubled, neither by spirit, nor by word, nor by letter as from us, as that the day of Christ is at hand. 2 Thess. 2:1, 2

Some were saying to the believers in Thessalonica that the Lord had already come, and it brought confusion. The believer has a full provision for safety in the abiding of Christ and the anointing of the Spirit. You don't have to be paranoid if you are rightly related in the body and rightly related to the Lord.

> And he that keepeth his commandments dwelleth in him, and he in him. And hereby we know that be abideth in us, by the Spirit which he hath given us. 1 John 3:24

> Ye are of God, little children, and have overcome them; because greater is he that is in you, than he that is in the world. 1 John 4:4

> Ye have an unction from the Holy One, and ye know all things. 1 John 2:20

> The anointing which ye have received of him abideth in you, and ye need not that any man teach you; but, as the same anointing teacheth you of all things, and is truth, and is no lie, and even as it hath taught you, ye shall abide in him. 1 John 2:27

This means that when truth is sounded, the Holy Spirit says Amen in our temple, and we either receive it or we struggle over it. If you don't accept it, you start to come out of His safety zone.

While standing in the middle of the battle I have listened to the thought of the enemy which tells me, "You don't know what to do," and I will agree with him, saying, "It is beyond my growth and maturity and experience. I don't have knowledge about it. I have never been in this situation before." Then I remember the Scripture that says I can do all things through Christ who strengthens me. Wait a minute! This isn't the right voice that is saying I can't do it. I have an unction from the Holy One and I know all things. I have the source of omniscience dwelling in me. He knows everything and rightly related to Him, I can call on His name. He can give me a word of wisdom or a word of knowledge. He can give me the tongue of the learned in season when needed and I can function and accomplish His will! I don't have to be bound by that lie!

When you go to war, you will face this battlefront and you will find that you are nothing in yourself; the enemy will make sure of it and God will allow it so you will learn how to be dependent upon Him. You will have to battle those lies. If you accept them, you will be overthrown, you will be dislodged from your position. Instead of saying, "I have to get there before I can battle," say "I am here. I am in Christ in heavenly places. I have the victory. I am in the victory and I function from the place of victory, and God, the Holy Spirit who created the heavens and the earth, will back me up!" You can do it if you walk with God, but make sure you are right with Him. The Bible says that if your heart condemns you not, you have confidence towards Him, and this is the confidence: to know that when you pray He hears you, and when He hears you, He gives you the petitions that you have asked of Him according to His will (see 1 John).

TARGETS OF THE ENEMY
TO LEAD OUR WALK ASTRAY

I pray not that thou shouldest take them out of the world, but that thou shouldest keep them from the evil. They are not of the world, even as I am not of the world. John 17:15, 16

As the days of Noah were, so shall also the coming of the Son of man be. For as in the days that were before the flood they were eating and drinking, marrying and giving in marriage, until the day that Noah entered into the ark, And knew not until the flood came and took them all away; so shall also the coming of the Son of man be. Matt. 24:37-39

Abraham was interceding with God and two angels of destruction for Sodom and Gomorrah while his nephew Lot was running around the city that day not even knowing that destruction was at hand. There are different levels of Christian living. Where are you?

And ye shall hear of wars and rumors of wars: see that ye be not troubled: for all these things must come to pass, but the end is not yet. For nation shall rise against nation, and kingdom against kingdom: and there shall be famines, and pestilences, and earthquakes, in diverse places. Matt. 24:6, 7

But before all these, they shall lay their hands on you, and persecute you, delivering you up to the synagogues, and into prisons, being brought before kings and rulers for my name's sake. And ye shall be betrayed both by parents, and brethren, and kinsfolks, and friends; and some of you shall they cause to be put to death. And there shall be signs in the sun, and in the moon, and in the stars; and upon the earth distress of nations, with perplexity; the sea and the waves roaring; Men's hearts failing them for fear, and for looking after those things which are coming on the earth: for the powers of heaven shall be shaken. Luke 21:12, 16, 25, 26

This know also, that in the last days perilous times shall come. For men shall be lovers of their own selves, covetous, boasters, proud, blasphemers, disobedient to parents, 105 unthankful, unholy, Without natural affection, trucebreakers, false accusers, incontinent, fierce, despisers of those that are good; Traitors, heady, highminded, lovers of pleasures more than lovers of God. 2 Tim. 3:1-4

Christians are *in* this world, but Jesus said we are not *of* the world. These references show what the world is like, but we are not to be partakers of its lifestyle. Our society has undergone a vast change in moral standards and mores, and we have the following as a description of what the enemy is creating in our world as drawn from the above Scriptures:

1. *Division* as exhibited by wars, nation against nation, and by racial unrest.
2. *Disloyalty*, as exhibited by betrayal, traitors, false accusers, even betrayal by parents and friends.
3. *Distress* as exhibited by persecution, hatred, prisons, putting to death.
4. *Degeneration*, without natural affection, unholy, incontinent.
5. *Debauchery*, that is lovers of self, money, and pleasures more than God.
6. *Dishonesty*, truce breakers.
7. *Depression* as exhibited by perplexity, hearts fainting for fear.
8. *Discord* exhibited by unthankfulness and disobedience to parents.

Throughout the early life of Christ the devil sought to tempt Him to swerve from the pathway to the throne by the way of the Cross. This is what happened in the wilderness temptation. This is what happened when He spoke to Peter about going to the Cross and Peter said, "Be it far from thee, Lord." However, Jesus defeated the tempter on every hand and became our sustaining victory; He became the INDWELLING, INCORRUPTIBLE LIFE in us. If we live by Him, then we can maintain our victory in Him! Nevertheless, throughout the pilgrim journey of the Christian, Satan will seek to decoy him from the victorious walk in the Spirit that God intends for him.

These Scriptures also show seven areas where the enemy seeks to overthrow us. The first area has to do with UNITY. Ephesians 4 says that we are to endeavor to keep the unity of the Spirit in the bond of peace. The enemy's effort is to bring division, to keep discord in the Body of Christ so that her power is dissipated and her effectiveness is destroyed. A divisive spirit is not of God.

Mark them which cause divisions and offenses contrary to the doctrine which ye have learned; and avoid them. For they that are such serve not our Lord Jesus Christ but their own belly; and by good words and fair speeches deceive the hearts of the simple. Rom. 16:17, 18

If you see divisionary people, correct them; if they don't receive correction, mark, and avoid them. That is a commandment, just coming next. Don't let the enemy break you off from the body! Keep your right relationship to the body and reach for those who are floating away. We are a family and have a responsibility to one another. We *are* our brothers' keepers and God holds us accountable.

The second area is a walk of HOLINESS, and degeneration is the contrast that the enemy tries to bring. The enemy will sift the life of a believer to find any weakness, such as a favorite sin. He will lay the trap to destroy your victory and your progressive development in the likeness of Christ by pressing you to get involved in that sin, and in so doing he will condemn you so that you become paralyzed and bound by the enemy. He often says, "Well, now you did it, didn't you? Ruined your life. Just couldn't handle it, could you? Just that one little, five-second thrill." Of course, beforehand he is saying, "Come on, it doesn't matter, it's all right. God understands that you are not perfect yet. You can go ahead and do it." God wants us to have a walk of holiness; without holiness no man shall see God, and the enemy wants to trap us with degeneration. If he can do that, then you are not effective in your warfare.

The third area is LOVE versus disloyalty. The Lord wants us to love each other. Satan delights in bringing fear and disloyalty by misunderstanding, misconstruing motives, misinterpreting words, or misinterpreting actions. As a result, we must guard our lives to avoid jealousy, envy, malice, slander, dislike, and backbiting. There are some safeguards in the Word. The Bible says not to receive accusation against an elder without two or three witnesses; and, out of the mouth of two or three witnesses shall every word be established. A witness is not one who wasn't there but heard it secondhand, he has firsthand information. Accept nothing without the two or three witnesses, and give the best possible construction on your brother and sister. If you are suspect, check it out. TRUTH ALWAYS STANDS UP UNDER INVESTIGATION. Assume nothing because your assumption will open a door wide for the enemy to work in the following way. "He didn't say 'Hi' to me. It must mean he doesn't like me." Maybe he was involved in thinking of something else, maybe his own life was in conflict at the moment, and WHEN YOU ASSUME, YOU OPEN THE DOOR TO THE ENEMY. Check it out. That is part of loving and being loyal to one another.

The fourth area is LIGHT versus distress. When we see the

light of God's truth, we find rest and peace. When we don't have truth in the battle, we have distress. We don't know what is going on and we are all torn up about it. The enemy loves to hide the sovereignty of God; he wants you to not recognize God's sovereignty or control in the events of your life. He wants to cloud the fact that God loves you and he wants to cloud God's purpose for your life. Many times a believer is in perplexity because he is blinded in the midst of his circumstances. Perplexity means no way out. The Bible says the Lord will not suffer you to be tempted above that which you are able but will provide a way of escape. *You as a Christian have a way out* .

Perplexity, then, is a non-Christian word. Sometimes it *seems* as if there is no way out, and I have been there. I have said, "God, I don't see You in this anywhere, but I know You are in control. You are here somewhere. You might as well come out of hiding! It is a little dark around here; would You shed some light on the subject? I know You are here, I know that You love me. I know that your purpose is at work and I refuse to accept anything else!" **I'M NOT DEALING WITH MAN AND I'M NOT DEALING WITH THE DEVIL. WHEN I WAS PURCHASED BY THE BLOOD OF JESUS CHRIST, I BECAME HIS AND ALTHOUGH I MAY RUN INTO MAN AND I MAY RUN INTO THE DEVIL, GOD IS ORCHESTRATING WHAT IS HAPPENING IN MY LIFE FOR HIS HIGHEST PURPOSES.** It is only as we hide the Word in our hearts that we can be assured of light to guide us on our pathway.

On a recent crusade trip to India, I was delayed entry into the country. I thought my crusade ministry to India was over and I went through distress. But I hung onto the truth I knew from God's Word which He had allowed me to experience on other occasions. I couldn't see Him in it but I knew He was there and I trusted Him, and it turned out that when it was all over the very thing that kept me in Delhi was not the enemy, but it was God's hand and through it He made a provision for me to stay in the country when the devil rose against us and would have had me deported. God was in it, but I didn't see it at the time. His Word says, "I will never leave you nor forsake you," and I had to stand steady on nothing but naked faith in the Word of God. That little bit of light relieved the distress.

The fifth area is WISDOM versus distraction. The enemy loves to take our attention from the Master to view one of his distracting circumstances. You can always see it happen when God is ready to do a wonderful miracle; that is when the demons act up. The flesh likes to do the same. It is done by some circumstance or display to abort God's purpose. In this way we are caught off guard and often sidetracked out of the mainstream of God's purpose in our life. You are on your way to a service and you really need the message that God is going to bring forth, and on the way you have a flat tire, your child starts acting up, everything goes wrong, and you say, "Forget it. I guess I'm not supposed to be in church today." We can miss God's provision by the distraction of the enemy's display.

The sixth area is PRAISE versus depression. A tactic of the enemy is to block the life flow of God in our lives by damming up the voice of praise. The enemy robs us of our gratitude towards God and leaves us crippled in our Christian walk. We can get so down on ourselves and into depression and ungratefulness for one reason or another that we dam up the life flow of God. Sometimes we say, "I don't feel like praising." What does that have to do with it? Your feelings are not your god. God's worthiness of praise is not changed because you do or do not feel like it. The humanistic attitude is do whatever feels good, but there has to be more to it than that. *You are to obey God's Word and worship Him because He is worthy, even when you don't feel like it,* and you will find the truth of the Psalm that says, "My mourning was turned in me to dancing." Victory comes because you offer the sacrifice of praise. He is worthy, whether you feel like it or not.

The seventh area is HARMONY versus discord. God wants us to have harmony, but by circumstance, by resistance, and difficulties the enemy seeks to bring discord. He often uses nagging, irritability, incompatibility, and indiscrete behavior. These kinds of things result in an estrangement between the brethren. The enemy wants to bring discord in your family and in the household of God. We should learn to be appreciative of the differences in one another: the abilities, the talents, the personalities, the gifts, strengths, and virtues. they may be very different from your area of interest, but that doesn't make them less valuable. We are able through Christ to keep the unity of the Spirit through love which covers a multitude of sins, and through His ability we are always able to triumph in Christ.

These are seven areas in your walk before God where the enemy will attack when you are involved in helping others in spiritual warfare, in your prayer life, in counseling, or ministry. These areas are those which I want to strengthen in my life and in the lives around me because I know they are stress points that the enemy will press against. I want to learn how to be understanding, strong, conscientious, and sensitive to these areas. This is part of being prepared for war, because if these are the target areas of the enemy, then we must protect them. If you are in a natural war and know the targets that the enemy is shooting at, then you put your artillery there. When you go to war with the enemy, you don't have to wonder where he is going to shoot. The Lord has already let you know; you have inside information, so do something about it. Strengthen the target area so when the enemy raises up his head, you knock it off! We should have enough wisdom to deal with those areas, to fortify them, and be ready for the enemy's attack and not to be taken by surprise.

To just learn about spiritual warfare is not enough. We must have application. The purpose of teaching about the Baptism of the Holy Spirit is to see people get baptized in the Holy Spirit. The purpose of teaching about water baptism is to see people baptized in water. The purpose of teaching things concerning spiritual warfare is so that we can become more effective in warfare, stabilizing our lives so we are less susceptible to the attacks of the enemy. We need to ask ourselves, "In these target areas of the enemy, am I in order in my life?" If not, you need to put them in divine order. At the top of the list is: having fulfilled your obedience to God. Then fortify your walk in the Lord in these seven areas. Make sure they are as they should be. Having made sure of this, know that the enemy will send things along to press in these areas, so put up some artillery, a Holy Ghost radar system so that you know how to identify things that bring division instead of unity, or things that bring disloyalty instead of love, or things that bring distress instead of light. Be prepared. Adjust your life, strengthen your target areas, be ready, as it says in 2 Corinthians, to revenge all disobedience *when* you have fulfilled your obedience. There is no reason for you to go away defeated.

Thank You for your Word, Lord Jesus. Come to our lives and by your Spirit identify for us areas that need adjustment right now, areas that need to be fortified. Help us, Lord. Teach us how that we can be strong in our inheritance and our position in You, so we can be consistent in our walk and be a blessing to others.

So far in this chapter we have examined two areas where the enemy wants to attack in order to overthrow our effectiveness:

1. Remove the Christian from his wealth as a believer, what you possess in Christ, that which is your inheritance. the enemy comes with doubt, disobedience, delusion, or deflection in order to get you away from that which you are in Christ—a new creation seated in heavenly places. If you don't know who you are, he will overthrow you. He will come along and say, "Jesus, I know; Paul, I know; but who are you?" If you say, "I don't know," he's got you. He gets you involved with disunity, discord, distraction from the proper priorities in your choices in the midst of the battle. As a result, you get ensnared and

pulled aside; you are involved majoring in the minors and minoring in the majors, and you miss the issue.

The enemy doesn't want you to be saved, first of all, but if you are saved and he cannot overthrow you so you lose your salvation, he will be content for you to be a Christian as long as you have no effect on anyone else being a Christian. As long as you say, "Lord, I'm just going to enjoy my salvation and I won't smoke or chew or run with those who do; I'll go to church on Sundays and that's all I'm going to do; but I'm going to be an ineffective witness because I'm afraid; I don't pray; I don't study the Word; I don't give financially or of my time or talents;" the enemy will not bother you. He has you where he wants you.

2. Lead the Christian away from his walk. God wants unity, the enemy brings division. God wants holiness, the enemy brings degeneration. God wants love, the enemy brings disloyalty. God wants light, the enemy brings distress. God wants wisdom, the enemy brings distraction. God wants praise, the enemy brings depression. God wants harmony, the enemy brings discord.

The Scripture says that we are not only to be sons, but we are to be soldiers in Jesus Christ. Satan is wanting to delay something. He realizes prophetically what Christians and the Word of God have been proclaiming, that there is a consummation of God's plan and his time is short. The Scripture says that in the tribulation period, when he knows his days are numbered, he really gets active. He wants to delay God's eternal purpose; he wants to avoid being cast into the lake of fire. He is in rebellion against God and trying to overthrow God's judgment.

In this age of grace, it is God's purpose to complete the Body of Christ. The Church of Jesus Christ will come to completion, God's purposes for the church will be finished, and the people of God will be conformed to the likeness and image of the Lord Jesus. They are to be prepared as the Bride of Christ, glorified and perfected in His likeness. The enemy wants to stop that. He will even allow the multiplication of a church in numbers as long as they remain spiritual babes and never grow up. Why? Because if they do not grow up, they will die out. Sooner or later they will drift into religion and lose out in their relationship with Christ. You cannot continue as a Christian without growing and not die spiritually.

The enemy tries to get us to become religious. All across America, the Harris and Gallup Polls indicate that two-thirds of the American population say they are saved Christians. That means there are many people who have been duped by the enemy. They feel they are all right with God, but the fact is they are headed for eternal damnation at the lake of fire. They do not have a vital living relationship with Christ and are not genuinely saved. It isn't enough to go to church on Sunday; you must embrace Christ as your Lord and Saviour and walk with Him and in His ways. There are many people in this country who think they are saved who are not, and that is an indictment against the church for failing to preach the gospel clearly enough.

DISABLE THE CHRISTIAN

The enemy is trying to keep us from entering into maturation, into God's purpose and effectiveness. In order to hinder the purposes of God and disable us as soldiers, there are three areas in which he works:

1. As the ACCUSER OF THE BRETHREN.

> And I heard a loud voice saying in heaven, Now is come salvation, and strength, and the kingdom of our God, and the power of His Christ: for the accuser of our brethren is cast down which accused them before our God day and night. Rev. 12:10

Accusation has a way of making us ineffective in warfare. It comes from without as well as from within. If you enter into warfare and pray with/for someone or counsel and share with them, the enemy comes along and says that God can't honor you because of the way you acted earlier in the day. Or he comes up with condemnation about something that happened in your past, before you were a Christian. "God can never use me because I was such a mess before I was saved." From within, he tortures you with remembrance of past sins and present sinfulness; he presses you with accusation in your mind until the realization of your failures, defeats, and mistakes, your weaknesses, and shortcomings, come upon you in such a way that you become incapacitated.

Who is the accuser of the brethren? Does Jesus accuse the brethren? Does He exhort us in His Word for the church to accuse the brethren? We are not to judge that other man, who is God's servant, because God is able to make him stand (Rom. 14:4). We must guard against the critical spirit.

Accusation takes place within ourselves, and without we meet the battle through emissaries who are at times God's people. Jesus said your enemy sometimes will be of your own household. Christians are not perfect, and at times the enemy uses them as he used Peter. One moment the Spirit of God was speaking through Peter, the next moment he gave voice to the enemy (Matt. 16).

The enemy will speak through us when we are not abiding in the Spirit. When you go to battle as a body and as a team, one of the things the enemy wants to do is to divide the members of the team through jealousy, envy, accusation, criticism, disunity, and disloyalty. Why? Because three in unity will be much more powerful than a man alone, and two together will be ten times more powerful (Deut. 32:30). Therefore, the enemy seeks to divide by suspicion, hurt, pain, comparison, and egotism.

The enemy uses jealousies, prejudice, hatred, or dishonesty. He will often flood a community or a group with whom we must deal with lies and false accusations in order to blemish the witness of a believer and discourage his faith. You may see a Christian woman with an alcoholic husband who may not be able to cope with his alcoholism all the time, and as a result she may get a little negative and frustrated and doesn't open her heart as well as we would like to see a Christian open her heart to her husband because of the hurt and the irresponsibility, selfishness, and sinfulness of that alcoholic husband. Pretty soon you find someone taking the side of the husband, saying, "The reason he's like this is because you're like that," not realizing that God's judgment of the matter is that the Christian woman who is struggling will find her place in heaven and the alcoholic will find himself in the lake of fire. We need to keep our perspective straight.

Accusation comes to accuse the righteous, to twist truth, and to make unrighteousness correct and get the issues all mixed up. This is one way the enemy hinders God's purposes.

2. As our ADVERSARY.

Wherefore we would have come unto you, even I Paul, once and again; but Satan hindered us. 1 Thess. 2:18

For a great door and effectual is opened unto me, and there are many adversaries. 1 Cor. 16:9

There are many ways to which Satan will resort in order to keep us from fruit-bearing service. I am going to mention some of them and you will recognize how the enemy has subtly thrown them at you and you will discover that it's not just a "little something" that you have allowed in your life. The moment you try to remove it, you find that all hell broke loose. Much of the time the enemy sleeps when he has us in a bondage that we aren't aware of. As soon as you begin to expose and correct it, he will resist you with all of his force. Such resistance is good confirmation that you are moving in the right direction—he doesn't resist nothing. If you are moving in a direction that will help his kingdom, he will not resist you; but if what you are doing in your walk with God is going to hinder him, he will try to shut you down.

The enemy will hinder you from going to a prepared place and people. Have you ever been praying for someone and they suddenly call, their heart is changed, they're open to the Lord, and you try to go to minister to that person? Every time you try to go all kinds of things happen to keep you from getting there. Satan hindered Paul from going to Thessalonica.

He will try to dissipate your time and strength. Someone calls you with a need and you say, "I'm really going to take that need before the Lord in fasting and prayer." You mean it, you are committed to it, you are sincere, but as you go to do it, someone takes their bicycle and runs it over your begonia; someone else breaks a front window; all kinds of distractions come and when you finally get it all taken care of and try to go to prayer, all of your strength and energy is dissipated and you are emotionally fatigued and not at your best for effective prayer. That is the enemy hindering you.

He tries to put such pressure upon you that you are so bound with stress and distracted that Christ's power becomes lacking. That is why when we go into crusades, I desperately need someone to go over and do setups and then to handle the many details during the crusade. I need to lock myself in for fasting and prayer and getting ahold of God. I can't be involved with all of those kinds of problems and have my mind and energy distracted, and then go out on the platform and see the kinds of results we have seen.

The enemy will get you so feverishly involved in activities that you are useless. In our crusade in Poona, India, some militant Hindus hired two hundred men to come to the grounds and destroy the meeting. God sovereignly intervened and prevented them from raising their arms at the signal. What happened? In the midst of this tremendous battle, I was hauled down to the police commissioner's office just before the meeting so that I could not concentrate on prayer. God gave me favor with the police commissioner and the meetings weren't cancelled. However, I could not stand in the gap as intercessor at that time, but back at home notice of the battle had been brought, the trumpet had sounded and people were fasting and praying twenty-four hours a day, and it won the victory. What would happen if the trumpet had sounded and everyone was too busy? "Well, I have to get my lawn mowed and I need to paint the eves and the shutters on the house. Maybe I'll do it tomorrow." Tomorrow would have been too late!

The enemy will occupy us with secondary and secular concerns; he will tempt us to use carnal instead of spiritual weapons. You get in the midst of battling in the Spirit for someone to get saved and you would just like to hogtie them and brand them and get them saved that way. YOU *WILL* RECEIVE CHRIST, you demand! But this is not God's way.

The enemy will intrigue you into worldly alliances and will tempt you to accept worldly counsel instead of seeking to know and follow the counsel of God. For example, God's plan of finance. Every day I get junk mail that says, if you will sell Grandma's light bulb, you can have money for your church project. I have never read in the Bible where I am supposed to get our church members to go out and sell light bulbs. That is an alliance with the world. The world couldn't care less whether the church prospers or not. They are just looking for some free labor in order to peddle their products so they can get fat off of our labor. That is not God's plan of finance! His plan is that we give from out of our substance tithes and offerings.

I have had people say that if only I didn't preach about certain subjects, they would really get in with the church and would help us financially. What a temptation! I know Madison Avenue techniques. I know how to get a pink envelope because that is the one which gets the best psychological response for money, and how to write to everyone who has ever been on a Christian mailing list and pressure them and use sob stories and emotional appeals to get money, but that is not God's method! A worldly alliance will lead you to spiritual destruction in warfare. I have seen some very well known evangelists whose families ended up in divorce and remarriage that has been inordinate and outside the will of God because their houses became vulnerable as a result of not going God's way.

There is worldly counsel that the enemy wants to bring to us instead of seeking to know and follow the counsel of God. We go to someone whose value structure is different from that of God's kingdom. The Bible says, "Walk not in the counsel of the ungodly," but we follow the counsel of the ungodly all the time, and when we do we become hindered by the enemy.

Every fresh opportunity to preach the gospel in a place which has been unreached *is challenged. Every true and powerful work of the Spirit will be cross-cut and counterfeited.* The enemy will do it to dissipate strength. Efforts will be made to close the door to the gospel in country after country. Right here in America we are in legal battles today to maintain our privilege of preaching the gospel of Jesus Christ.

3. As a PERSECUTOR AND MURDERER. Jesus speaks very tactfully to the Pharisees:

> You are of your father the devil, and the lusts of your father ye will do. He was a murderer from the beginning, and

abode not in the truth because there is no truth in him. When he speaketh a lie, he speaketh of his own; for he is a liar, and the father of it. John 8:44

And they overcame him by the blood of the Lamb, by the word of their testimony and they loved not their lives unto the death. Rev. 12:11

Right now, in country after country, there are men of God who are in prisons and concentration camps, some being tortured because of being Christians. I know areas of the world, including India, where people are stoned for preaching the gospel. We aren't used to that kind of persecution because we live in a country that has been established on biblical principles of government. Although they are being twisted in this hour, we have been a bastion of hope to the world and have known a freedom that has never been known before.

We must recognize that we are in a war, and because we are enjoying liberties, we cannot forget our brethren who do not have such liberties. We have a responsibility to them, and as we seek God about that responsibility we recognize that torture, persecution, resistance, attacks, disease, and disaster are all part of the Christian witness. Nevertheless, God has given us the key for victory. You and I can have victory in the face of these kinds of adversaries, but that victory is won in the spirit world where, in the authority of Jesus Christ, the power of the enemy is bound and corralled inside a boundary and he cannot break out except in divine purpose. That is where the battle is won.

How do you win the battle in the spirit world? Three things are mentioned in Revelation 12:

(1) *They overcame him by the Blood of the Lamb.* How? Why? What is so important about the Blood? When we become a blood-bought Christian, we are in covenant relationship with God.

I don't believe we understand the power of covenant. Our country and culture have been so perverted from the truth, commitment, and honesty of God that we cannot comprehend it. You and I cannot go out and just have a verbal agreement with someone and expect them to keep it. We must have all kinds of written legal contracts and if everything imaginable isn't incuded, you will possibly be cheated. Even then, although you have a written document many times someone breaks it and you are still left without recourse.

This is the kind of society we live in. Therefore, we don't understand covenant and we don't understand contract from God's viewpoint. But God says this about His Word in Psalm 138: He has magnified His Word above all His name. At the name of Jesus every knee shall bow and every tongue confess that Jesus Christ is Lord, and He has magnified His Word above all His name. Psalm 24 says, "Who will go to the mountain of the Lord? He who has a clean heart, clean hands, *he who swears to his own hurt and changes not."* How important are covenant words to God? Not one dot over an "i" or a cross of a "t" will fail until all is fulfilled. His Word is settled forever in heaven. Heaven and earth will pass away but God's Word shall never pass away.

Joshua, although deceived by the Gibeonites, entered into a covenant with them. God told him not to do it but he did it anyway (Josh. 9). Until this day God has required Israel to honor that covenant because He wants us to keep our word. That is why Jesus said, "Let your communication be Yea, yea; Nay, nay; for whatsoever is more than these cometh of evil" (Matt. 5:37).

When God gives a promise, He means to keep it; you can count on it. It is more reliable than life itself. Abraham entered into a covenant with God for himself and for his progeny. This is an example of a three-party covenant. Because Abraham was faithful to keep his part of the covenant with God, God was obligated to keep His part of the covenant to Abraham's seed regardless of what that seed did. The Scripture says that God wants to be known forever as the God of Abraham, and His faithfulness to His covenant with Abraham is seen even in our generation by the regathering of the nation of Israel. God's supernatural intervention in their behalf is read daily in the newspapers and is a *TESTIMONY TO GOD'S FAITHFULNESS TO HIS COVENANT PROMISE.*

God is faithful, and that means something to me. When I go to war, I have to have something to stand on because when all hell is thrown at me, I want to have a place that is secure. I want to know I'm going to come out on top. That place is covenant relationship. Jesus said, "This is the new covenant in my blood." "All the promises of God in him are yea, and in him Amen (2 Cor. 1:20). Every new covenant promise is yours. When you meet all the conditions, you can count on the blessing. he says, "If ye abide in me, and my words abide in you, ye shall ask what ye will, and it shall be done unto you" (John 15:7). If your heart condemns you not, if you are in right relationship with the Lord and your fellow man, then you have confidence towards God, and this is the confidence: that when you pray you know He hears you and if He hears you, He grants the request according to His will (1 John 3:21; 5:14, 15). The Scripture says if any two of you agree touching anything in heaven or in earth, it will be given to you of the Father which is in heaven (Matt. 18:19).

"If ye shall ask anything in my name, I will do it" (John 14:14). *Asking in Jesus' name means that you have come into union with*

God's priorities, God's methods, and God's motivations, and whatever you ask in unity with God's priorities, methods, and motivations He has said that He will do. There are thousands of unfailing promises in the covenant of the blood—and they overcame the enemy by the blood of the Lamb making that covenant commitment. I'm going to live for You 100 percent, God. I'm in the place where my heart doesn't condemn me, your Word abides in me, I am abiding in You, and I'm disciplining myself. That means I can ask because I have allowed You to deal with my motivations, with my priorities and with my methods, so that I am in harmony with You. From that position I have the promise of God that says, "Delight thyself also in the Lord; and he shall give thee the desires of thine heart" (Ps. 37:4). And God, who is not a man that He should lie, is faithful to perform it, for He says, "I will hasten my word to perform it" (Jer. 1:12).

I have studied what this blood covenant means and I stand on it. When I go to war, I say to the enemy, *"I've been bought with the blood; I have a blood covenant; I am right with God, I've checked it out according to His Word, not your accusations, and now, in the authority of the name of Jesus Christ, the resurrected Son of the Living God, Satan, be thou bound!"* And all the power of heaven is released to make that devil obey. You are in a position to overcome; if you are not in that position and you step out against the devil, he may overcome you. Sometimes you find out what your weak spots are when he knocks the wind out of your sails.

(2) *They also overcame by the word of their testimony.* We overcome the hindrances of the enemy, and the spoken Word of God sets on fire the course of nature. No matter what comes to you, the promise of God is that all things work together for good to those who love God and are called according to His purpose. God will supernaturally intervene in all things no matter what the enemy throws at you, no matter what kind of trick he tries to pull. God says that He will make that circumstance work together for eternal good in your life and in the Kingdom of God *if* you are obedient to Him and walking in His purposes (Rom. 8:28). There is always a condition. If you love Him, keep His commandments. Love is a giving word, and Jesus translated love into terms of behavior. Love is obedience to the revealed will of God.

When you are in the correct position, the Word of God is powerful. There are two words in the Bible, "logos" and "rhema", that are translated from the Greek as "word." "Logos" is the general Word of God, the "rhema" a personal Word of God spoken to you by the Holy Spirit. There is no other way you can have a rhema in your life except that the Holy Spirit sovereignly speaks it to your spirit. When He does, that rhema is the source of faith; the discovery of God's will is the beginning of faith. When you have come to the place where you doubt your doubts and have overcome the contradictions of the natural world and have come to a place of full assurance and confidence in your spirit in that Word from God, then you can speak it and as a Christian rightly related to Him, that Word spoken in faith will have creative power. The Bible says, "The power of life and the power of death are in the tongue." He says, "I create the fruit of the lips." "The tongue sets on fire the course of nature." They overcame by the word of their testimony. They spoke the Word and weren't silent. They not only had the blood covenant, but they used the Swod of the Spirit which is the rhema of God!

(3) They also had an attitude of commitment which said they *loved not their lives unto death.* The worst thing that can happen to you isn't a broken arm or getting into an auto accident and becoming paralyzed. The worst thing that can happen to you is death. You can't go any further than that. When you are resurrected from the dead, you will receive a great healing because everything is wrong with you when you are dead!

The Scripture says that men walked in the fear of the devil and the fear of death which was in the power of the devil until the resurrection of Christ. Men were bound all their lives. But now as Christians we are no longer bound by the fear of death because death has no sting. Christ has tasted death for every man, and WHEN YOU COME TO A TOTAL, FULL COMMITMENT, YOUR LIFE IS IN GOD'S HANDS AND YOU ARE READY TO LIVE OR DIE FOR CHRIST. To die for Christ may be a lot easier than to live for Him. If this commitment isn't in your heart, the enemy will search out that which you put above God. What do you love most? When you get down to the point where you are tested with your life, where your priorities are manifest, if God is not the number one priority in your life, something else is.

Jesus said in John 14 on the night that He was betrayed, "The prince of this world comes and he has nothing in me." There are times in your life, especially in warfare, where the prince of the power of the air will come and, by the spirit of the enemy, examine your life, your heart, your priorities, affections, and motives, and if there is something that is not Christ-centered which he finds in you in the middle of the battle, he will use that as a hook or ring in your nose and will pull you to the downfall.

But these overcame because of the Blood of the Lamb, by the word of their testimony, and because they loved not their lives unto the death. When the prince of the world came, he sifted their hearts and he had nothing in them. Judas was brought down. Saul was brought down. But those whose heart was fixed towards the Lord stood and overcame. You have a key for victory: by the Blood of the Lamb, by the word of your testimony and by not loving your life to the death.

Finally, my brethren, be strong in the Lord, and in the power of his might. Eph. 6:10

Combining this Scripture with 1 John 4, which says, "Greater is he that is in you, than he that is in the world," you know that you wrestle from a place of victory. It says in 2 Timothy 2:1, "Thou therefore, my son, be strong in the grace that is in Christ Jesus." Christianity isn't for namby-pamby weaklings, for fearful, yielding back-peddling people. WE ARE TO BE STRONG. We are to never fear or falter or faint, but we are to always be prepared with an enduement of fresh strength enabling us to be victorious from the start to the finish. You can run way ahead of everyone else in a race but if you fail to cross the finish line, it does not matter how well you ran.

I once heard Clara Grace speak towards the end of her ministry. She was a prophetess and a mighty woman of God. She talked about a recent vision that she had had. She saw Jesus working on a beautiful table in a carpenter's shop. Over on the side was a big book, the book of her life, and it was turned towards the end. He brought her to that book, showed her a couple of things in it, and left immediately for John's baptism. She said the Lord let her know she had one more cross to go through in her life, and that it would be the hardest of all. She said that the greatest trials are at the end of your life, because the devil does not want you to finish the race.

I have seen various movies traveling back and forth on airplanes. I was impressed with one movie of a fellow who was going to run a marathon in the Olympics, how he slipped on something, fell and knocked himself out cold and got up hours after everyone else had finished. He had been running well and something happened that tried to knock him out of the race, but he got up and ran until he finally came into that arena and across the finish line. Although it was just a worldly movie, God talked to my heart through it. Here was a man who was down, but he didn't quit because he was strong. There was something about his spirit that made him press on. All that mattered was that he was going to cross the finish line, and people watched him and cheered as he did. It is like the great cloud of Christian witnesses who are watching your life. They want you to finish.

You have an enemy who is going to try to stop you from finishing, and when I read that phrase, "Be strong," I think of the need to cross the finish line. Don't falter or faint until the finish. You are not a quitter. There are times when you feel like quitting in the battle. You get faint, you get tired, you can't take another bit of resistance and you don't want to go on, but you must go on!

Every great athlete has learned to press himself when it hurts, and that is what makes him great instead of mediocre. The Scripture likens the Christian walk to a race and to run as if one would win, and you are to press. It is not always comfortable to press, but life isn't made out of what is comfortable. Be strong, because the enemy wants you to quit, to fall short.

After World War II, Winston Churchill stood as the strength of England, having led that country in the midst of terrible war, in the midst of being destroyed, and kept that country's spirit and led it to victory. He was brought back to his alma mater to bring a graduation address and as he stood up, he said, "Never, never, never give up. Never, never, never give up. NEVER, NEVER, NEVER GIVE UP." And he sat down. He had given the secret of England's strength. When the Scripture says be strong, it means to have the kind of spiritual strength, commitment, and effort that when you lay your hand to the plow, you don't look back. He that lays his hand to the plow and looks back is not worthy of the Kingdom of God. The Scripture says that whatever you do, do it heartily, with ALL YOUR HEART! Nothing less is worthy of our Saviour and His Kingdom!

The victory is ours when we realize that strength is first of all in our inward attitude. To assume power or authority, we must be assured of power and authority, but that assurance will never come if we look at ourselves or at the enemy. This is why the Scripture says the joy of the Lord is your strength, and that is why one of the weapons of warfare deals with worship and praise. This is the will of God concerning you in Christ Jesus, that over and above everything you give thanks. KEEP YOUR EYES ON THE LORD, KEEP YOUR EYES ON THE KING OF KINGS; GET YOUR EYES OFF YOUR INADEQUACIES AND THE IMPOSSIBILITIES OF THE TASK, BECAUSE WITH GOD NOTHING SHALL BE IMPOSSIBLE. When you get your eyes on Him, you keep your focus straight, you keep your worship and your heart straight and you don't get distracted. *Your faith will rise in your heart as you look onto Jesus, the author and the finisher of your faith, and you become strong and assured*—not of yourself, but knowing that you can do all things through Christ that strengthens you. Then you are in a position to go to war. Be sure you are ready. When you go to war, you want to be strong. When all falls around you and there is no one who stands with you, you are not alone because you stand in the strength of the Lord Jesus Christ. Though a thousand fall at your left side and ten thousand on your right, it will not come near you.

The kind of thing I'm talking about is personal in your relationship with God. You have to settle these issues yourself.

You can't have someone else do it for you. When you want to get saved, no one else can believe God for your salvation for you. You must accept God and believe Him. If you want to be baptized in the Holy Spirit, no one else can do that. You have to get a hold of God and believe Him. When you want to go to war and be strong, you must pay the price yourself. Either you press in and get the goods or you go without. God is not a respecter of persons, but He is a rewarder of those who diligently seek Him, and if you will draw near to Him He will draw near to you, and if you don't have the goods it is because you failed to pay the price! Let's not excuse it with anything else. Let's not blame the preacher, let's not blame the church, let's not blame our parents let's not blame our job, let's not blame our spouse. IF YOU DON'T HAVE THE GOODS, IT'S BECAUSE *YOU* FAILED TO PAY THE PRICE. If you want the power, authority, and strength of God, you have to pay the price yourself. There is no other way. You must make that trip up Mount Calvary, die, and rise again in newness of life.

OUR STRENGTH LIES NOT IN A METHOD, NOT IN A TECHNIQUE, BUT IN A PERSON, AND THAT PERSON IS THE LORD JESUS CHRIST, at whose name every knee will bow and every tongue confess He is Lord to the glory of God the Father. Jesus Christ is our strength. You can learn all about Him without knowing Him. You can know all the principles that He taught and walk in perfect obedience to all those principles and not have the power of His might because you don't know Him. BE STRONG IN THE LORD, not in your will power, not in your talent, intelligence, abilities, finances, or heritage. *BE STRONG IN THE LORD.* That means you have to cultivate a relationship with Him. Jesus said, This is everlasting life: To know the one true God experientially by participation and interaction (John 17:3). How do you know about Him? You know about Him in His Word but as you walk in His Word, it leads you to Him. Jesus said of the Pharisees, "You search the scriptures for they testify of me, but you would not come to me that you might have life" (John 5:39, 40).

How often in the midst of your struggles do you read a book, find a verse of Scripture, go talk to a pastor and get counsel, understanding, and direction, but you don't go to your knees and really get a hold of God? You talk about it and you talk about it and you talk about it some more and yet you have never really pressed through and gotten a hold of God. He is a rewarder of those who diligently seek Him. Not always in your own timing, but if you seek Him wholeheartedly and diligently, He will meet you, and that is where your strength is. Unless we meet with Him and are clothed with Him afresh before a battle, we cannot stand.

Counsel is helpful; studying the Word and finding out the principles is helpful. But when you get all of those things done, you still have to go to Jesus. *He is the only way; there is no other.*

We have seen that the enemy in this third area where he is trying to attack us does so as the accuser of the brethren, as our adversary and as the one who is our persecutor and murderer, spiritually or physically. We overcome by the Blood of the Lamb through blood covenant, the word of our testimony by getting the rhema of God and walking in it and speaking it, and because of an attitude that we love not our lives unto death. We *endure.* Jesus Christ is the same yesterday, today and forever. You don't have to wait for Him to get in the right mood to approach Him. He is always the same, and when you mature into the likeness and image of Christ, you are no longer on the roller coaster of up and down, on and off, but you are the same, you are stable, you are enduring, you are consistent, again and again and again, and you never give up because you have found your strength in the Lord!

Father, bring us to total commitment, teach us of your ways, and bring us to your feet that we may have LIFE. Grant the grace of your Spirit that is needed so that each one can find your strength in his life.

9

Be Strong in the Lord

Finally, my brethren, be strong in the Lord, and in the
power of his might. Put on the whole armour of God,
that ye may be able to stand against the wiles of the
devil. For we wrestle not against flesh and blood, but
against principalities, against powers, against the rulers
of the darkness of this world, against spiritual
wickedness in high places. Wherefore take unto you the
whole armour of God, that ye may be able to withstand
in the evil day, and having done all, to stand. Stand
therefore, having your loins girt about with truth, and
having on the breastplace of righteousness; And your
feet shod with the preparation of the gospel of peace;
Above all, taking the shield of faith, wherewith ye shall
be able to quench all the fiery darts of the wicked. And
take the helmet of salvation, and the sword of the
Spirit, which is the word of God: Praying always with
all prayer and supplication in the Spirit, and watching
thereunto with all perseverance and supplication for all
saints. Eph. 6:10-18

There is much that is implied by the phrase, "Be strong in the
Lord," and one of the implications is that we are weak. There is a
tendency to be weak in warfare; otherwise, we would not have to
be exhorted to be strong! An inherent necessary truth that you
and I must be aware of in order to be effective in warfare is our
personal weakness. Spiritually, we do not have the capacity or the
strength in ourselves to resist the powers of darkness.

Paul said in Romans 7, I know that in me, that is my natural
flesh, in my natural man, there is no good thing. If you aren't
convinced of this in your heart when you go to war, you will make
a detrimental mistake. Unless you are convinced of your
ineptitude, you will meet a situation in warfare which you will try
to handle in your own way or in your own strength or ability.

Failure is a good way to progress in the Kingdom of God.
When you fail, you find out what you don't have and it is good for
your humility and for your being teachable. You will then
recognize that in war you must have divine enablement, that
Jesus is your source. He is your wisdom. He is your strength. He
is your authority. He is your power, and He is your ability. You
learn to cling to Him, especially when you know how desperately
you need Him as your source. Being convinced of your weakness

is a very important factor in spiritual warfare. You must know, not just in your head but in your heart, that what you are in yourself is not enough.

Many times we will acknowledge intellectually that the Lord is our source, but when a circumstance comes, instead of checking with the Lord and submitting our response to Him, we gut-level respond to the circumstance according to what we think is going to handle the situation. If this is our reaction in warfare, the enemy, being as clever as he is, will set us up again and again and we will have the same kind of failure. In fact, repeated failure of a certain kind is an indicator that you are walking in your own way and your own strength. That failure is a good teacher so you can advance in the Kingdom of God by recognizing that you are walking in your own strength and learning to turn to the Lord.

Before I came to the Lord, I had been tremendously deceived and had led people the wrong way by the influence of my life. When I became a Christian, I said in my heart, Lord, I am never going to speak to anybody ever again about spiritual things. I didn't want the responsibility. No one was going to hear about this! Well, when the Lord calls, you have to obey if you want to keep your relationship with Him. I realized how susceptible I had been and I have never again had confidence in my own ability. Immediately after I got saved the Lord began to teach me about *spiritual safety*. There are things that I have followed all through the years of my walk with God that have kept me in a place of confidence in my relationship with Him. Not confidence based upon my ability to discern or my faith or my obedience to God, but a confidence that comes because I know what God says about safety and I have followed it. I trust His integrity and I trust His Word to keep me when I follow His directives.

Be strong *in the Lord,* don't be strong in yourself. Be weak in yourself in the sense that you are recognizing your weakness, recognizing your susceptibility, recognizing that the enemy might have misled you, recognizing that you might have misread the circumstances, and always being in a position to allow the Lord to adjust and correct your perception and your response. Once the Lord has confirmed what He is saying to your life, STAND. But you must come to that strength in God.

In being strong, I feel there is an implication that we are not to fear. Many times people meet the enemy and they become afraid. I remember Martin Luther's illustration. In the middle of the Reformation when the enemy was attacking him, he woke up one night and saw the devil personified at the end of his bed. Many people would go, "Ohhh, where's the pastor?" But Martin Luther said, "Oh, it's only you," rolled over and went back to sleep. He knew who he was in Christ and he knew that as long as he was rightly related to the Lord and to His people, the enemy had no power over him except the Father gave it to him.

I was amazed at the grace of God when we were in Poona, India, in 1981. There was a report that there would be a violent attack to disrupt the meeting and our lives would be in danger. I told the police commissioner there would be no attack, that there would be perfect peace. When I first walked out on the platform, I thought there might be certain things in my message that night which I could compromise in order to keep from stimulating the crowd into violence, but I looked at my interpreter, told him we weren't going to back off a bit and told him to be sure to say exactly what I said. We came against the problems and God gave us a total victory. And I was amazed at the fact that I was not afraid.

God gives us a holy boldness, and when the Word says to be strong, it means you must come to a place where you overcome fear. The opposite of fear is confidence, and the Bible says this: If our heart condemns us not, then we have confidence towards God, and this is the confidence: that when we pray, we shall ask what we will and we know that He hears us and if He hears us, He will give us the petitions that we have asked of Him (1 John 3:21, 5:14, 15). I had made sure that I was in the right place with God, and I was able to be strong in the Lord because there was a confidence in my heart, my heart having been searched by the Spirit of God and condemning me not.

When you go to war, then, *you have to make sure that you are rightly related to the Father and to your fellow man.* If you have some things that aren't right, take care of them because they will open the door to fear and to lack of confidence; you will wonder if God can honor you or back you up because of what is wrong in your life. You will be in a place of doubt instead of faith and the enemy will gain access in the circumstance.

Being strong, then, knows not only our own weakness, it knows our strength in the Lord. It means that we don't falter or faint—we continue. There is a tendency in the middle of the battle when the going gets tough to back off, to want to quit. Usually that comes just about the time of the breakthrough. In my own experience with God in war, I find that I am stretched to my outer limits of capacity and as that happens, there always seems to be something that the Lord would like to adjust in my life. GOD'S NUMBER ONE PRIORITY IN OUR LIVES IS CHARACTER FORMATION INTO THE LIKENESS AND IMAGE OF CHRIST, AND EVERYTHING THAT HAPPENS IN YOUR LIFE IS A TOOL THAT GOD USES TO BUILD YOUR CHARACTER. Unless you recognize that and respond accordingly, you are not rightly relating to your life circumstance. So in the middle of warfare, as I find myself coming to the end of my strength and capacity and call upon the Lord for more strength, wisdom, and direction, He always pulls out the little carrot and says, "Son, do you see this in your life?" Oh, yes, Lord, let's just put that away. "No, if you let me have this, then I'll give you the victory." That happens to me over and over again and brings me to a place of desperation, but in that place things happen. God changes me as I surrender, and He gives the victory. I believe that is why we sometimes come to the place where we are about to falter and to faint before the victory comes, because God is using that kind of desperate circumstance to get at something in our life which, because of our lack of understanding, stubbornness, or ignorance, has been hard for Him to reach.

So *being strong implies coming to the end of ourself, at which point God will intervene by bringing a change in us and then the victory.* We also learn that BEING STRONG MEANS TO BE EMPOWERED OR PREPARED WITH AN ENDUEMENT OF FRESH ANOINTING SO YOU CAN BE VICTORIOUS FROM THE START TO THE FINISH. We are to go from strength to strength. They that wait upon the Lord shall renew their strength, and if we are going to be strong in the Lord, then we must wait upon Him. "And they shall mount up with wings as eagles, they shall run and not be weary, they shall walk and not faint." *To be strong, we must learn to wait on the Lord and be renewed in strength.* To go to war without spending proper time waiting on the Lord and disciplining ourselves to do so is to cause ourselves to meet defeat.

Victory is ours when we realize that strength is first of all in our inward attitude, the battleground being the mind. Never, never, never give up. We must learn an attitude of strength. To assume authority or power, one must be assured of authority and power, but that assurance will never come if we look at the enemy instead of looking to the Lord. If we look inwardly we will faint; if we look outwardly at the circumstance, we will faint; *we must keep our eyes on the Lord from whom our strength comes.*

We learn that our strength lies in the person of Jesus Christ, not in a principle, not in a method, not in a technique. Many times when we go to war, we have a little technique or method that we may have learned, but that will run short in the battle. *The victory comes as we gain our strength through the person of Jesus Christ.* We must allow the reality of His presence to come and minister to us and be manifested and released through us by the Spirit. The Scripture says that the presence of God will be as a defense for us, illustrated when Israel came up out of Egypt. As they came to the Red Sea, Pharaoh and his men behind them, the manifest presence of God came as a cloud that was a fire that kept the children of Israel warm and as a fog that blinded the Egyptians so they could not find the children of Israel until God opened the Red Sea and sent them across on dry ground. The presence of God made manifest was a defense, and we need that reality. Not a principle. *A principle should lead us to a PERSON, and as the PERSON is manifest in the situation, His manifest presence is the defense.*

We are also to *be strong in the power of His might;* our strength must be seen in Him. We see His authority and the power in His miracles; we see His righteousness and victory over temptation; we see how He met sin and the powers of darkness; how He met political opposition; how He met the opposition that came from His own disciples' unbelief; how He dealt with circumstance after circumstance. We recognize the power of His might as manifested in His life, and realize that our strength and power in war is not just in who Jesus is but also what He *has. He has the victory already!* Our part is confident assurance of power over all the power of the enemy. CHRIST AT CALVARY TOTALLY AND COMPLETELY DEFEATED THE POWERS OF DARKNESS. There is no exception, and you and I as we walk with the Lord have this testimony from Him: "Behold, I give you power over all the power of the enemy and nothing shall by any means hurt you" (Luke 9:1, 10:17). When we are in the right place with God and we appropriate our place of authority by faith, then we have victory, and WE ARE TO COME INTO WARFARE FROM THE PLACE OF VICTORY, not from the place of needing to gain it. We enter the warfare as victors through faith in the victorious Lord, and we must keep our eyes fixed upon Him.

For you to have the power of His might, *you must be fed in your Spirit regularly.* If that doesn't happen, then you will become spiritually anemic and susceptible to disease, attack, and failure. You will have very little resistance. That is why it is important to be in church services, to study your Bible, to pray, to be in fellowship, and to be strengthened in the inner man.

In the old days of war when they used swords, the Scripture talks about a time when their hands would cleave to the sword. They would hold it and wield it in the battle, and by the end of the battle their hand would cleave to the sword to the point where they would have to peel the hand off the sword. That took a lot of physical energy. If you were a general in a battle of that nature, one of the things you would do is make sure that your army didn't go to battle hungry, without food for three or four days and being weak and unable to wield the sword and unable to stand in strength and endurance. If you wanted them to produce, if you wanted them to be enduring, if you wanted them to be strong and be assured of the victory, you would make sure they had been well fed. That is why a great tactic in that kind of warfare was to cut off the supply lines, and that is one of the things the enemy will do in your warfare. *He will seek to break the supply lines: he will break your fellowship; he will break off your source of spiritual food; he will get you distracted and involved in something else to weaken you, and then having weakened you, he will set you up for the attack.*

We must also exercise. It says in Hebrews 5 that strong meat belongs to them who by reason of use have exercised their senses, to be keen in discerning good and evil. If you don't regularly pray, read the Word, and share Christ with people who are lost, then you will be flabby spiritually. You won't have endurance or strength. I found that true in college when I had stopped exercising, and one day some in-laws came into town and we went to a park for a picnic and decided to play a little game of football. It wasn't five minutes and it was heart attack time, and I wasn't even thirty years old! I began to realize that I had to start doing some kind of exercise. If you don't exercise your spiritual senses, then you aren't going to be able to be effective in warfare. Milk belongs to those who are unskillful in the Word of righteousness. You need to be skillful in the Word. You need to apply the Word to your life and to your circumstances, through prayer, study, witnessing, involvement in Christian service, and intercession. You must develop a sensitivity to pick up the enemy's subtlety or it will creep in and by the time you discern it, you are already trapped and you have lost the battle, and if you lose too many battles you lose the war.

We also need discipline.

> Know ye not that they which run in a race run all, but one receiveth the prize? So run, that ye may obtain. And every man that striveth for the mastery is temperate in all things. Now they do it to obtain a corruptible crown; but we an incorruptible. I therefore so run, not as uncertainly; so fight I, not as one that beateth the air: But I keep under my body, and bring it into subjection: lest that by any means, when I have preached to others, I myself should be a castaway. 1 Cor. 9:24-27

Paul said that although he preached the gospel to others, he kept his own body in subjection lest having preached to others he himself should be a castaway. He said that all those who run the race are temperate, they are under discipline and control, lest they would beat the air and run in vain. He said run as though one would win and used a picture of athletics. What happens if you are going to be involved in some athletic contest? You must develop your abilities, you must discipline yourself. If you are a swimmer, then you will develop techniques by the way your hands enter the water and pull them out, and the way you kick so that you lose the excessive drag, and you learn to develop and strengthen your muscles with exercise that will bring endurance. You develop techniques on how to turn so you can do it quickly and efficiently. You practice and practice, and the one who does the best job is the one who wins.

You discipline yourself to keep your attention on what you are doing. A swimmer trying to keep inside his own pace, who has developed his body to go at that pace, gets hung up because he is watching the guy in the other lane and begins to compete with him, and it throws him off. He must keep his attention on what he is doing if he is going to win.

These principles are true in warfare. We need discipline. Sometimes we go to church and walk with God the same way we go to a job. We go in, put in our time, and come home and sit back and relax. In Hawaii, they would have a war, suddenly call the war off and have games fo a few months and then they would go back to war. That usually doesn't work if you have a really mean enemy! The devil won't go away and leave you alone until you are ready to get back into the fight. You can only quit when the victory is won, and that takes discipline to endure, to stand, to continually pay attention, not to assume that it is all okay but to continually watch and to know the victory is won.

When you go to war, you need tu enter into covenant relationship and remember the promises of God. You can stand on His Word. I don't care what's happening around you, I don't care how much of hell Satan and his emissaries can be throwing at you. All hell can break loose, even the earth that you are standing on can give way beneath your feet, but if you get ahold of the truth of God and are in a place where you have *met the conditions of faith and obedience,* and if you put your feet spiritually on the Word of God, heaven and earth will pass away but God's Word will not. He means what He says and he will confirm His Word with signs following in your life. Because THE ENEMY knows that, he WILL TRY TO GET YOU TO STAND ON SOMETHING OTHER THAN THE WORD, A TECHNIQUE, A FORM OR APPROACH, AND HE WILL TRY TO DISCOURAGE YOUR CONFIDENCE IN THE WORD OF GOD.

It was a wonderful testimony to watch my mother-in-law when she had a pinched sciatic nerve. She went to the hospital in a lot of pain, unable to walk, and the doctors said they would have to do dangerous surgery or the leg would shrivel and she would never be able to walk again. She believed the Lord to heal her and said she wouldn't have the surgery done, and the doctor walked out on her and refused to take responsibility. A physical therapist told her that because a certain thing was happening, it meant her nerve was already dying. But she fought all of those testimonies because she had the promise of God and being the woman of faith that she is, she set her faith on God's Word. It didn't matter what medical science said, it didn't matter what the feelings in her body were telling her, it didn't matter what she could or could not do, the only thing that mattered was the Word of Almighty God. Today that woman walks all over the place, even pulling weeds out in the garden—which was what caused the nerve to be pinched in the first place—because she had faith in the Word of God regardless of what anyone else said! She didn't get anything instantaneously. She quotes a favorite Scripture: As the day is, so shall my strength be. Yes, I'm better today. Feel any better? No. Can you move your leg anymore? No. Pain just as much? Yes, but I'm better today, because God has promised to heal me. When you go to war you need the kind of tenacious faith that lays hold of the Word of God and doesn't rely on what any other source says: *God's Word is reliable.*

That is war, and sometimes it is difficult when everything around us tells us no and the only thing you have to hang onto is the Word of God. The Scripture says that we are to be strong in the Lord and in the power of His might. Why? THAT YOU MAY BE ABLE TO STAND. You need to have these things; without them you won't be able to stand. With these things, you will be able to stand against *ALL* the wiles of the devil, anything that he can throw at you. Notice our part: If we have met these preconditions, we are to stand still and see the salvation of the Lord who shall fight for us.

It is wonderful when the Lord lets us see some of what He does. After the crusade in Poona was over and we were heading for the court area, the man who had hired all of those Indian nationals to storm the platform came running up to me, waving a written retraction he was going to put in the paper. He said, "I know that you are a man of God. When all two hundred of us came onto those grounds, none of us could raise our arms!"

When you are strong in the Lord and in the power of His might, and He enables you to stand, then you see the salvation of God. The Lord gives us the victory; He is the one who fights. We have to wrestle and we have to stand, but He is the one who will bring forth the victory. We are to *stand in the perfection of Christ's finished work;* we are to *stand in our divinely appointed position in Him;* we are to *stand when* we are seated with Him *in heavenly places far above all principalities;* we are to *stand in the position over all principalities, over all powers, over all dominions;* we are to *stand against Satan in Christ.* The enemy is under our feet and we are not to wrestle *for* a position of victory, but we are to wrestle *from* a position of victory. The moment you wrestle for a position of victory you are already defeated. We are to **STAND UNCONQUERED.** We are to stand our ground in the day of battle and having fought to the end, come off victorious on the field, standing invincible.

We are to put on the whole armour of God. In this armour of God, there is only one offensive weapon, and that is the sword. The rest is defensive. There is no retreat in the battle. War involves blocking out the offensive blows of the enemy and landing some offensive blows of our own, and we are to put on this armour of God as our power, as our authority and position, and it is all in Christ who is our protection.

There are six pieces of armour listed in Ephesians 6, each of which is a source of strength and security in warfare:

Truth

The first one that is listed says, "Stand, having your loins girt about with truth." The implication in the King James Version is that someone girds you, but the implication in the original language is that you gird yourself.

When you go to war, there is nothing more obvious than truth being the only authority. God will never back up that which is not truth. Sometimes truth is hard to find because the enemy wants to distract, cloud, misguide, and misinterpret. The Bible tells us that out of the mouth of two or three witnesses every word is established. Our loins, a place of strength in battle, must be girded with truth. Jesus said, "I am the way, the truth, and the life. No man comes to the Father but by me."

Truth is not a precept or a concept. *Truth is a person*, and this is very difficult to understand intellectualy, but the Lord has taught me that it is true. Proverbs says that the plowing of the wicked is sin (Prov. 21:4). Plowing the field is a good thing to do if you are a farmer raising your own food. Yet the Scripture says that doing good when you are not right with God is sin. Good works without being rightly related to God are deceptive to solving the conviction of the Holy Spirit and one's sense of guilt by rationalizing that you are a good person instead of allowing the conviction for sin to work and bring genuine repentance and right relationship with God. Good done by the wicked is a very subtle form of deception.

You might have someone sharing from a position against what God is doing and the point that he is making seems to be correct. But because his relationship with God is not right, his point is wrong. For example, I have had many people ask me about good works organizations, like feeding the hungry. I believe feeding the hungry is something that Christians should be doing. We have responsibility in our abundance, but I don't believe Christians should contribute to organizations that feed the hungry without giving the gospel. You feed a mass of starving people without giving them Christ and they will still drop dead after a period of time and go to eternal damnation.

God never works for time; the humanist does. God always works for eternity.

To feed that hungry person is a good thing to do, but to do so without doing it in the name of the Lord is deceptive, and in our society, because of that very principle, we have an ethic that says that if we are just getting along with one another, that is all that matters. Whatever seems good is fine as long as you don't violate whatever someone else wants to do.

How does that relate to feeding babies? When you feed the hungry without giving the gospel, you do it by sapping the financial strength, talent, and energy of the Body of Christ. Instead, we should feed the hungry in the name of Jesus, giving the gospel as well, for eternal results. God calls the wicked doing good works evil. The one appears as truth, but there is no Jesus in it, and Jesus is the truth. When the person of Jesus isn't in it, truth isn't in it.

The enemy will try to trick you with subtleties of lies.

And to the angel of the church in Philadelphia write; These things saith he that is holy, *he that is true*, he that hath the key of David, he that openeth, and no man shutteth; and shutteth and no man openeth. Rev. 3:7

I have no greater joy than to hear that my children walk in truth. 3 John 4

Unity is built around truth. Unity built on a lie will never last. Jesus said, "If you are not for Me, you are against Me." It is either the Lord or it is not. Sometimes we don't always know, and at such times we are vulnerable because we have no place to stand. "Stand, having your loins girt about with truth."

The soldier's girdle here wasn't just an ornament. It went around the body and it held together all the pieces of the armour, in a way that would also give the soldier freedom of movement. This divine girdle of truth must encompass our whole life and that truth must be applied. When you deal with an issue where the enemy is working, truth is what sets you free. The surgeon's knife may wound, but it can help you. The truth may wound, but there is healing in it.

Some things are easy to receive, but there are some things that you struggle with. I struggle with certain kinds of truth that come to my life because they cross against things that I want, and I must die. You have to die to self and to your own direction in order to embrace Christ. When truth comes, it will release you into freedom. But we are bound by lies that we think make us free. The enemy keeps you from seeing correctly, and as a result of this deception you don't respond correctly. Deception doesn't have to do so much with a heart condition. Many people come into salvation from cults and we can put our arms around them and love them, tell them that God loves them and it's all going to be okay, but love alone is not enough. the *truth* sets you free. The answer to error and deception is truth. They need to be loved, but if you really love them you will give them the truth.

When you have an area where you don't know the truth and you believe a lie, your heart is sincere but you are blinded and your responses are inappropriate, only as truth is manifest are you set free. One of the enemy's most favorite tactics is to cause you to blame him for that for which you are responsible. You condemn yourself because you haven't accepted yourself in Christ. You haven't accepted that you are a new creation. Someone comes along and says, "That's just the devil," so you go around rebuking the devil and there is no progress. Your heart is perfectly sincere, but nothing is really answered because the fact is that *you* are condemning yourself.

On the other hand, you have someone who is not condemning himself, but a spirit of the enemy has come and has been accusing him as the accuser of the brethren. He thinks he hasn't forgiven himself, that he is condemning himself, so he is running around trying to find out what is wrong in his life, when all he needs to do is take authority over the enemy.

The outward behavior of these two examples seems to be the same, but the sources are different, and the enemy has you when he can confuse the issue like that. Even though your heart may be sincere, you are ineffective because you are bound by deception, and the only thing that will set you free is truth. When the truth comes under the anointing of the Holy Spirit, God backs it up. When you embrace the truth, it sets you free; when you reject the truth and excuse yourself, you come under the corrective dealings of God. Our loins must be gird around with truth for us to be effective in warfare.

The Breastplate of Righteousness

The breastplate covers our heart: the affections and the desires, the thoughts and the intents of the heart. They need to be protected. Feelings follow behavior. In our society, we have been taught that behavior follows feelings. "I did that because I was angry." Well, why were you angry? Because your behavior was wrong in the first place—you responded incorrectly to something. An obvious example in the Scripture tells us there is no peace for the wicked, but when you come to Christ there is peace. Obedience to God's command of repentance brings peace;

disobedience brings the wrong feelings. If you want to get rid of the wrong feelings, you need to correct the behavior, the feelings follow. The Scripture says that the fruit of righteousness is peace, and righteousness defined behaviorally in the Bible is obedience to the revealed will of God out of a heart motivation of love. So God reveals His truth and will; you are obedient to Him because you love Him, and it brings the fruit of peace. If you think right, talk right, and act right, you will feel right.

Wrong desires, wrong ambitions, and wrong affections are tools that the enemy will use to ensnare you in warfare. In order to protect those areas in your life, you must wear the breastplate of righteousness, the breastplate of obedience to God's revealed will. If you find yourself continually vulnerable in your desires, it tells you that you are not properly wearing the breastplate of righteousness. It tells you that there is some area in your life where you are not obeying the will of God, and when you go to war you must be obedient or the enemy will bring you down. You must have the correct loyalties, priorities, affections, and desires. When you are vulnerable to the attack of the enemy and are being overthrown by him, and when your affections and desires are led astray, it tells you that your breastplate isn't working. You have some things that are out of order in your behavior, attitude, thoughts, actions, and speech. Go to the Lord, make the correct adjustments, your affections and desires and motivations will come into line and you will have a defense that the enemy won't be able to break.

At this point in this study, I believe God has been speaking to your heart. Some have yet to discover how to be strong in the Lord; some have been weak and haven't been willing to recognize and acknowledge their weakness so they have been walking in their own strength and finding failure; others have recognized their weakness and have been trying to be strong in the Lord but have been getting hung up with methods and techniques instead of coming into the PERSON of Jesus Christ, who is their strength. Some, in seeking to do that, have discovered that they are anemic from lack of spiritual food, or maybe their exercise hasn't been as it should be, or they need to lay hold of the promises of God. They want to put on the armour of God but they have not put on truth in certain areas of their lives. They have been vulnerable.

If you find that you are unable to stand and be strong, it is because there is an area where truth is not operating and you need to find truth in that area where you are struggling—God's truth in the person of Christ. You may be having difficulty with your affections and desires, and your heart towards the Lord isn't as it should be. It is because the breastplate of righteousness isn't on and it needs an adjustment. You need obedience worked into your life. It might be that you haven't been obedient because of ignorance. Nevertheless, right behavior will bring right feelings; it will bring the breastplate on your affections.

You need to acknowledge these areas if God has shown you that you lack in them. Something will change inside as soon as you do and you will start making progress in areas where you previously struggled.

Heavenly Father, right now we thank You for your Word. We thank You that your Word set us free because it is truth and it is alive. It is sharper than any two-edged sword to the dividing asunder of soul and spirit and is a discerner of the thoughts and intents of the heart. Father, for every area that has been touched by You, I pray that You will bring light and understanding and bring an adjustment as we commit those areas to you. Father, I pray that we will be strong in the Lord Jesus Christ and in the power of His might, that we will have put on the whole armour of God, having our loins girded about with truth and having put on the breastplate of righteousness. Lord, confirm your Word in each of our lives with signs following for Jesus' sake, Amen.

10

Shod With the Gospel of Peace

He is our peace, who hath made both one, and hath broken down the middle wall of partition between us. Eph. 2:14

My peace I give unto you: not as the world giveth, give I unto you. Let your heart not be troubled, neither let it be afraid. John 14:27

When we think of the peace of God and of our feet shod with the gospel of peace, there are a couple of areas that we must focus on. One is obvious: our relationship with our fellow man, especially in war. The enemy knows the old adage of divide and conquer and he wants to bring division, distortion, suspicion, and disloyalty that will divide the strength of the army of Christ. He brings things to stir up strife between us: rumors, accusations, slander, misinterpretations of events, etc.

If you are keeping on the breastplate of righteousness, you will also be making sure that there is nothing you are doing that would contribute to a lack of peace in your relationships. You will be making sure that those relationships are put in divine order and that you are walking with integrity, love, and righteousness. You cannot give that which you don't have; you cannot share what you have not as yet partaken of. If you are going to share the gospel of peace as an outreach, you must be a partaker thereof. So in your own relationships, the peace of God needs to be at work, and when that is not happening, you are susceptible to the attack of the enemy. As soon as your relationships are not as they should be, the enemy will accuse you in that area and your faith will go from the top to the bottom and you will not stand in confidence.

You cannot stand well if your feet are not properly shod. If you don't have the right kind of shoes for the terrain, you may step on a thorn. Firemen have special boots with steel plates in the bottom so when they go through a burning building that is falling apart, they don't drive nails so easily into their feet. They have to be prepared, and so it is in war. A well-equipped army has certain kinds of combat boots and equipment that will protect them in the terrain in which they will do battle. We find here it is being shod with the gospel of peace.

Making sure our relationships are right is absolutely vital to effective warfare. If we have a relationship that is out of divine order, it will be a means by which the enemy will gain access and attack us.

There is a peace that we need when we go to war. There will be things we will face that in the natural way can be very frightening, and we need the peace of God. As soon as you find fear entering in, it will destroy faith. The enemy always works in an atmosphere of fear; that is his environment. We find that God lives and abides in an atmosphere of praise of His people. The praise and worship of God's people is an expression of love, so *God, who is love, moves and lives in an environment of love.* The Scriptures say that *faith works by love.* When He says, "Let not your heart be troubled, neither let it be afraid," we must recognize that *fear is a tactic of the enemy to disturb our peace, to stimulate doubt and unbelief.* You are afraid that God is not going to keep you; you are afraid that you are not going to get the victory; you are afraid that something terrible is about to happen. The enemy comes with fear to disturb your peace, and if you allow fear to come in, then you will be overthrown. But if you have the peace of God and are abiding in the love of God, it will stimulate faith. You will find that in peace you have confidence and you stand still.

There is no such thing as just being afraid; you must be afraid of *something.* What are you afraid of? You are afraid that something contrary to God's Word will come to pass. Warfare gets right down to whom you are going to believe, whom you are going to turn to. Are you going to believe the Word of God or the enemy? "By his stripes we are healed." "These signs will follow them that believe: they shall lay hands on the sick and they shall recover." "Whatsoever you ask in my name, I will give it to you that the Son might be glorified in the Father." "If you abide in me, and my words abide in you, you shall ask whatsoever you will and it shall be done unto you."

Suppose you have cancer and you have all of these promises of God telling you that you can receive your healing in victory and deliverance. Then the doctor tells you that there isn't much that can be done except that through medical know-how, they could allow you to live two or three more years. And they charge you everything you could earn for the next thousand years, and you can leave that bill as a heritage to the taxpayers or your family and in the meantime they can prolong your misery. We appreciate everything that medical science can do, but when you get right down to the tough questions of life, medical doctors can't do very much.

When you are in a situation like that, fear comes and you have a struggle. The enemy says you are all washed up, but God's Word says to ask what you will and it shall be done unto you. And you walk through the valley of decision, and in that valley you choose between faith and fear, the lie of the devil or the truth of God. The decision should not be difficult, because the devil is not a reliable source! I wouldn't build my life on his word; I would rather hang my life on the Word of God that is confirmed by five immutables. He backs up His Word, so you know that He means what He says, He says what He means, and He performs what He said He would do when you have met the conditions He has set forth.

God knows that we meet all kinds of situations in life that will rob us of the peace of God through inward distress of spirit and mind or affections. Only the peace of God will be sufficient for our hearts in the midst of the losses of life or the infirmities and tragedies that we all face. When we walk through a disordered world, there are a thousand things to bruise and wound us, but the peace of God that passes all understanding will keep our hearts and minds through Christ Jesus. We need a supernatural peace. We need that which comes from God. *Our* peace alone is not enough to stand in the battle. There are tragedies; there are things that should not happen that take place because of sin, or because once in a while we just miss God. The enemy gets a good lick in and when that happens, we are knocked flat for a minute. We are not forsaken, but it does bruise. That doesn't mean it won't heal, but it is a tragedy and in crises we need the peace of God that goes beyond our natural abilities and understanding.

The exciting thing about the peace of God is that it is independent of your circumstances. It is a fruit of the Spirit, and when I have the peace of God in my heart, it is because of the fruit of a personal relationship with Him. If my wife were to leave me or if my children were killed in an auto accident or if a doctor told me I had cancer of if the church burned down, in my heart I would still have the peace of God because it is independent of the circumstances in my life. The peace of God comes out of my relationship with Him, and that is why it passes all understanding and why it will keep my heart and mind. The fruits of the Spirit have nothing to do with my circumstances.

All of us find joy and peace when our circumstances are as we would design them. Use your sanctified imagination and design a circumstance that would be picture perfect, but it would all be empty if the Lord wasn't there. You discover that the peace we are talking about has nothing to do with whether the circumstance is as we want it or if it is the worst circumstance we could imagine. How do you find this supernatural peace? "Rejoice in the Lord always: and again I say, Rejoice" (Phil. 4:4). Are you rejoicing in the Lord Jesus Christ? That is the first condition. You must be a worshiper; you have to joy in the Lord; you must love Him and magnify His name.

Let your moderation be known unto all men. The Lord is at

hand. Be careful for nothing; but in every thing by prayer and supplication with thanksgiving let your requests be made known unto God. And the peace of God which passeth all understanding, shall keep your hearts and minds through Christ Jesus. Phil. 4:5-7

Every time I find someone whose peace is destroyed, I take him to this verse and tell him these are the things we must do to have the peace of God. Where are you not doing that? "Oh, I haven't been praying; no, I haven't been worshiping. I don't feel like it." Remember, feelings are the result of behavior. Do what God says, and you will get the results that He says. When you begin to rejoice in the Lord, you will find that the peace of God will follow.

When you go to war and your peace is disturbed by the slightest little thing, you may lose your faith and come into a place of fear and the victory will be lost. So we need to have our feet shod with the gospel of peace.

The Shield of Faith

Above all, taking the shield of faith, wherewith ye shall be able to quench all the fiery darts of the wicked. Eph. 6:16

Faith is an interesting word. One of the things that it does is connect the soldier of Jesus Christ with the Master, the all powerful, the all sufficient Lord whose victory over Satan is total and complete. That victory is ours, but it must be appropriated.

I think of the fiery darts as the thoughts and circumstances that the enemy throws into situations, and they need to be quenched by faith. It says in Hebrews 11:6 that without faith it is impossible to please God. That means faith is vital and you cannot be effective in warfare without it.

I am so glad that what we have in God is built upon faith and not upon ability, whether it be creative talent or intellectual or athletic ability. I'm even glad that it is not based on good looks! A little child can work the works of God, while your Ph.D college professor at times will struggle over them, because they are by faith.

How limited is faith? Jesus said, "With man it is impossible, but with God all things are possible to him that believes." "According to your faith, so be it." "As you have believed, it shall be."

What can you believe for? For many Christians, faith is like a mirage, something you always see out there but never get to. Many Christians struggle finding faith. Faith is defined in Hebrews 11:1, and it can be said three different ways: Now faith *is*; now *faith* is; *now* faith is. Faith is something that exists in the present. Faith will never exist in the future, it will never exist in the past. When you look to the past, you are looking at belief

140

because it is all over and done, history. When you look to the future, it is not yet made manifest and is something that is *hoped* for. But faith always operates in the present. You might believe that someday God will do something for you; that is hope. God did something for me; that is past. If you are going to receive something, you will have to receive it in a moment of time, in a place that God has created for this dispensation called the "now." You got saved and baptized in water in the now; you got baptized in the Holy Spirit in the now; you got healed in the now and you touched God for your unsaved loved one in the now. Much Christian preaching is for the future and for the past and that is why it doesn't lead people to God. You must deal with what He is doing for those people in the present. We can talk about faith all night for the miracle service that is a few weeks away, but if we say, all right, Jesus is present right this moment to heal, we are in a different ball park. We struggle with all of our doubt and unbelief and everything that is in conflict in our spirit because we want to push it off to the future or the past; it is not like us to deal with it in the present because faith is foreign to us. What is normal to us is unbelief which, according to the Bible, comes out of a sinful heart. Unbelief is sin, just as adultery and stealing and murder are sin.

When you start struggling for faith, it is just like peace: you must make a choice of whether to believe God or the enemy. As you are in the middle of the battle of faith, you need to learn to put your doubt somewhere, and you will either doubt God's Word or you will doubt the enemy's word. Since your natural man tends to doubt God because he is born in sin, you should LEARN TO DOUBT YOUR DOUBTS AND PUT YOUR FAITH IN GOD.

"Faith *is* the substance of things hoped for, the evidence of things not seen." The word "substance" here means to substantiate, to bring into substance. The faith that is in the now brings into manifestation the thing that was hoped for. You will hope and begin to pray and believe God for the salvation of your loved one or for your healing or financial breakthrough, and you intercede until you come to a place of faith and believe God, and as you believe God it is settled in the spirit. You take it in the Spirit before it is ever manifest in the natural. That is why it is faith, because once it is manifest you no longer need faith; *between the prayer and the answer is when faith is manifest*. If it is just hope, nothing is brought about, but if it is faith, by definition it does bring into manifestation, and if it doesn't do that then it isn't what the Bible calls faith. As soon as you touch God in genuine faith, it is yours, it is settled. There will be time between the moment you believe God and the time it is manifest, but it will come. That kind of faith in your heart is the evidence that what

141

you have not yet seen but believed for will be manifest.

"Through faith we understand that the worlds were framed by the word of God, so that things which are seen were not made of things which do appear" (Heb. 11:3). If you want to understand, you must have faith. Did you know that God's Word is more solid than the earth you walk on? The real substance of this world is in faith. All of the rest is temporal.

Romans 4:17 states that God calls those things that are not as though they were. He calls you the righteousness of God in Christ! In faith you contact Him and the creative Word brings into existence that which did not appear. When God spoke the word that you are forgiven, life was birthed in your spirit, and that life has been working in you to transform you, until it comes to its desired end of making you into the likeness and image of Jesus Christ. That is why He can call those things that are not as though they were because what He says will be brought to pass. That is the nature of God. someone said that when Jesus came to the grave and said, "Lazarus, come forth," if He hadn't called him by name all of the dead of all generations would have come forth! THERE IS POWER IN HIS WORD!

Faith is not resident in you and I; we don't have any in ourselves.

For by grace are ye saved through faith; and that not of yourselves: it is the gift of God: lest any man should boast. Eph. 2:8, 9

You didn't even have faith to be saved. You were saved because God in His grace gave you the gift of faith. The Scripture says that God has dealt to every man a measure of faith. It says in Hebrews 12, "Looking unto Jesus, the author and the finisher of faith," the one who initiates faith and completes faith. Faith has a beginning and a completion. It has its beginning as you look to Jesus and discover God's will; it has its completion when it is brought fully into manifestation.

Jesus is the living Word. If faith is initiated in Jesus, then it is initiated in the Word. Romans 10:17 says, "Faith cometh by hearing, and hearing by the word of God." What is the Word of God but the revelation of God's will? Therefore, FAITH COMES WITH THE DISCOVERY OF GOD'S WILL. Do you have some kind of physical ailment? Do you believe that God is willing to heal you right now? If you really believed it, it would be manifest. There is nothing magical or superspiritual about it; the moment you believe it is yours.

We can teach and preach about it in order to exhort others to come to a place of faith to receive. That is why God sometimes works through the Word of Knowledge in a miracle service because that word encourages our faith. It shocks us out of our unbelief. You can receive the moment you believe in genuine faith. The problem is we don't have faith to receive because we aren't *really* sure that God wants to do it right now. That is unbelief.

Is it God's will to heal you right at this moment? "I don't know. I know He can, I believe He will some day. Right now, I like to think so, but I don't know." And the "I don't know" puts you in a place where you cannot have faith. I can't pray for someone and believe God to heal him if I don't know if it is God's will to do so. How can you ever pray for anyone in faith that God will heal him if you don't know that it is God's will to do so?

Faith begins in the discovery of God's will. If you knew that God wanted to heal, that He is able to and He genuinely wants to do it right now, you would not have a hard time believing Him to do what you knew He wanted to do. *The written Word is the declaration of the Will of God,* so understanding God's will is the beginning of faith. Faith does not have its origin in man; it has its origin in God, and we begin to receive faith when we discover and understand what God's will is.

When you go to war and you are meeting a situation and having to believe God as you intercede, and you are not sure what God's will is in that situation, you cannot battle in faith because you are struggling with unbelief, confusion, and doubt and the enemy overthrows you with his fiery darts. You need to know the will of God for that individual, for that moment, for that situation, because if you don't, you are shooting in the dark!

Many people don't want to pay the price to know the will of God, so they walk in generalities. Generalities are good principles to test specifics, but they will never give you specifics. You can test a specific: "God has called me to Africa." Is that scriptural? Yes. You have God's way of testing guidance: your elders, the Word, the witness of the Spirit, circumstances. You have the general principles to test the specific leading to see if it is the will of God, but you can take all of those general principles, memorize and quote them, and they will never give you a single specific. It can just as easily be God's will for you as far as the general principles are concerned to never go to Africa in all your life. You need to know the will of God for you. Faith has its origin in the discovery of God's will. When you don't know what His will is, you cannot move in that area with faith; you will have doubt, hesitation, and an incomplete assurance.

When the Word of God comes to us, it does not always produce faith in the beginning. Our response generally is hope. God speaks to us and we say, "Oh, I hope so. I want that to be true. I want to believe that." That is why the Scripture speaks of faith as that which brings into substance the thing hoped for, and because genuine faith finds its origin in the discovery of God's will; hope develops into faith as you continue to press into God. That is why VISION IS ALWAYS GREATER THAN FAITH; the Scripture says that people without a vision perish. In a more literal translation, "Without a vision the people will cast off restraint" (Prov. 29:18). They will cast off the necessary discipline, pressing, effort, and aggressiveness, for the Kingdom of Heaven suffers aggression and the aggressive take it by force. YOU MUST HAVE A VISION. YOU HAVE TO BE PRESSING FOR IT. It is not a hope-so attitude, but as you press in, faith begins to unfold as the will of God is manifested, you lay hold of the vision by faith and it begins to be brought into manifestation!

Jesus gave us the ordinance of the Lord's Supper, the ordinance of water baptism, the principle of the laying on of hands, and anointing of oil for healing. There are no other ordinances or rituals He gave the church. When you don't have the goods because you don't know the will of God, when all you have is generalities but not the reality of faith, then you have to talk about the Kingdom but never manifest it. If you really walk with God, you will have to come into a genuine discovery of His will and as you do, it will bring hope and as you walk in that hope it will bring faith. *If it is genuine biblical faith, it will produce that which is hoped for.*

You cannot go to war without faith, for without faith you don't have the protective shield, you don't know what God's will is. When God reveals His will to you and you know exactly what He is saying and it is confirmed and established, you are walking with full assurance in His Word. It doesn't matter what the contradiction of the natural world is. It doesn't matter what the impossibilities are as far as nature is concerned. It doesn't matter what the accusation of the enemy is. You can walk through hell on that Word and *nothing* will turn you aside.

You have to believe the Lord. This brings an excitement, but at the same time it brings a certain anxiety because you don't always know what God's will is. If you don't know, the first thing that you need to know is that you don't know. Jesus said the sick seek a physician. If you don't know you are sick, you never seek a physician. You must know enough to know what you should ask for.

So if you are going to quench the fiery darts of the evil one by faith, you must learn that the initiation of faith is in the Word and the discovery of God's will, and that Jesus is the completer of faith. Endurance is a word that many of us in America have thrown away. We have been taught about a walk with God through the Four Spiritual Laws and other simplistic concepts.

There is more to it than saying, "Jesus, come into my heart, forgive me of my sins, I accept You as Lord and take my life." In fact, theologically it can be demonstrated that you *are* saved when you receive Christ; as you walk in this life you *are being* saved; and if you continue and endure unto the end, you *shall be* saved. If all you have is one tense of this, you miss two-thirds of salvation. Jesus is the finisher. The Scripture says that of Him and through Him and to Him are all things to whom be glory. It begins to Him, is carried out through Him and is finished under Him. faith needs to be brought to completion.

> Looking unto Jesus the author and finisher of our faith; who for the joy that was set before him endured the cross, despising the shame, and is set down at the right hand of the throne of God. For consider him that endured such contradiction of sinners against himself, lest ye be wearied and faint in your minds. Heb. 12:2, 3

You have not resisted unto blood striving against sin. You think you have it tough? How many times have you been taken out and stoned for preaching the gospel? How many stripes have you been beaten with because you have given a Christian testimony? "Ye have forgotten the exhortation which speaketh unto you as unto children; My son, despise not thou the chastening of the Lord, nor faint when thou art rebuked of him" (Heb. 12:5). The rest of this passage deals with the chastisement of the Father, that every son whom He receives He scourges and chastises. This has to do with the finishing aspect of faith. I call it the carrot-on-the-stick approach. The Lord is wanting to take you from where you are now to where you are to be, from the image of Adam to the image of Christ, and in order to motivate you He allows circumstances to come in which He has promised to meet those needs and desires. He gives you promises; you discover His will; you believe Him for it; you start walking down the pathway of faith; and He says, "That's right, son. However, if you want the carrot on the end of the stick, you have to be changed. This thing in your life has to be removed." *Between the prayer and the answer, God makes saints.*

I have learned in my walk with God that if I want His blessings in my life today, I must have a higher walk of holiness than I had yesterday. You meet a circumstance and you want the victory; you press in and understand the things of the Word and of faith; you believe God, and He says, "It's yours, BUT that has to change in your life." And you say, "Oh, Lord, anything but that!" Then you dig in your heels and insist there has to be some other way to get around this cross. "I want resurrection ground, I want that table spread before me in the presence of my enemies, I want to say 'glory to God!' in this resurrection life, but I don't want to go through Calvary to get there. Anything, but don't let me die." But He says you must die in order to be resurrected. It is part of the finishing of faith. He always puts it out there and says, "All right, come this way a little." He gives you a little carrot and then puts another one on the stick; you want some more and you come a little farther.

He knows your nature. He knows what is in the heart of man. The Bible says there is none righteous, no, not one; there is none that seeks after God. So He creates in you divine motivation. It says in Philippians that it is God that works in you to will and to do of His good pleasure. He lets you taste a little of the heavenly gift, you want to abide in that place, but certain things have to go in your life. You see the Christian who refuses to give up smoking—he never goes on into what God has for him. He has lost the vital flow; he is not eating the carrot because he never moves from Adam to Christ. That means he doesn't walk in the reality of faith. He may be saved in the past tense but he is struggling with really being saved, and if he continues to struggle with being saved, he won't endure to the end and be saved. *You can have Jesus as Saviour only for a little while unless you have Him as Lord in your life. You must allow Him to deal with you, to change you.*

If we are going to have the shield of faith when we go to war, we must recognize that God will have to see us changed in order for the enemy to be defeated in war. As we go to war and overcome the enemy and obtain things by faith, we lay hold of God's provision and He will change things in us. When I first got saved, I was so excited! I wasn't going to be like the children of Israel; I was going to get out in the wilderness and there would be just a straight path to the Promised Land! That is not what I saw when the Lord took me into the wilderness—I saw two heel marks being dragged all over the sand. That is our nature, and when it happens to you don't feel like you are the only one. There is no temptation but what is common to man.

Faith, then, has this finishing aspect and if we are not willing to embrace it, we will not see the finishing faith. *Endure.*

Now no chastening for the present seemeth to be joyous, but grievous; nevertheless afterward it yieldeth the peaceable fruit of righteousness unto them which are exercised thereby. Heb. 12:11

CHANGE IN US BRINGS COMPLETION OF FAITH.

Father, you see each one who needs to know your peace, not the peace of the world that is dependent upon circumstance, but your peace. Let the peace of God that passes all understanding just permeate their beings right now, in the name of Jesus. Let that peace begin to settle every thought and bring it into obedience to Christ. Jesus, You are not only the Author of our faith but You are the Finisher, the One who brings it to completion. Lord, we know through your Word that it is your desire to change us between the prayer and the answer, and that we are not to cast away our confidence which has great recompense of reward but to know that after we have done the will of the Father that we might receive the promise according to your Word. I pray for each reader, give them a new vision, a new perception of Jesus as the finisher of their faith. Lord, give them an inner strength to endure and to do the will of God. May that which they have believed You for, that which they have discovered is your will and that which they have laid hold of by faith be brought to completion, for Jesus' sake, Amen.

11

The Helmet of Salvation

And take the helmet of salvation . . . Eph. 6:17

For who hath known the mind of the Lord, that he may instruct him? But we have the mind of Christ. 1 Cor. 2:16

In several places in the Scripture it says, "Let this mind be in you which was also in Christ Jesus." In other words, we are to allow the mind of Christ to be in us and we are to be renewed in the spirit of our mind. The mind of Christ might be bottled up with all of your carnal thinking because the natural man and the carnal mind are enmity against God and are irreconcilably opposed to Him. Your natural mind cannot know the things of God; they are spiritually discerned. To your natural mind the things of God will seem foolish, but after the Spirit you will be in awe of the majesty and the authority and the fullness of the things of God.

Positionally, we *know* that we have the mind of Christ, and as we mature, experientially we have the mind of Christ. There are organic problems that can occur with our minds so that we have difficulty with speech or visual perception, but those are not intelligence problems. For years scientists used to think that deaf-mutes were really stupid because they couldn't communicate, until someone finally learned to communicate with them. We find some of our most intelligent expressions of creativity have come from people with handicaps. You do not have to have ignorance and stupidity operating in your life. You can have the mind of Christ! and if you have the mind of Christ, that means that as you walk in Divine Purpose, you will walk with a supernatural intelligence, with a supernatural ability to perceive, to understand, to be able to discern, and to creatively work with your situation. The Bible says that the Spirit of God will bring to your remembrance whatever He has spoken to you (John 14:26). Your recall ability, therefore, becomes perfect in the realm of the mind of Christ.

A.W. Tozer was a great man of God who was trying to help bring a real flow of the Spirit of God in the Christian Missionary Alliance church. One thing he said was that the difference between the man who was speaking truth and a prophet of God is this: a man can speak any old truth that he decides he wants to talk about, but the prophet of God is the one who speaks the truth that God is speaking to those people at that time. To have the mind of Christ is to know what God is saying and doing in a situation.

God demonstrates a certain degree of approval by revealing His mind to us. That is why you talk about the mystery of godliness and the hidden things of God. Sometimes you try to share the most simple things with a person and he cannot comprehend it. Not because there is an intelligence problem; he may have four or five Ph.D's and may be able to understand physics and how to send a man to the moon. But you talk to him about the simplest concepts of christianity and he cannot comprehend it because of a spiritual problem. When we have the mind of Christ we have an edge, we have a perception and an understanding, an ability to relate to the world. That is why Christians go to the top. Every society that has turned to the gospel of Jesus Christ has been like cream and the generations that followed went to the very top. A society that has turned from God and has begun to go after their own minds begins to sink and deteriorate. Study world history in relationship to what is happening in the church and what is happening to God's people, and you will find the rise and fall of nations is a perfect parallel of their response to the true and living God. Only where the gospel is preached have you ever needed a patent office. There hasn't been creative intelligence at work in a society outside of the influence of the gospel.

The Bible tells us that we are to be renewed in the spirit of our mind and to have the mind of Christ, and we need the helmet of salvation. This has something to do with our head, our thinking, our mentality. We need protection over our mind in war. As a man thinks in his heart, the Scripture says, so is he. Whether you are right or not, *you will relate to God according to your concepts.* We must realize that God is greater than our concepts, and the person who will not accept that will not walk in the supernatural power of God because he has to reduce God to his carnal mind.

But God is greater than your ability to conceive. With all of the accumulation of knowledge through all generations, man still has not found out how the tomato seed actually grows and produces a tomato. The intelligence of man is as nothing to God. WHO HAS KNOWN THE MIND OF GOD THAT HE MIGHT INSTRUCT THE LORD? We come with such haughtiness in this generation with the little bit of knowledge that we have accumulated and we think we know so very much, but you should be glad that God is greater than your concepts because your concepts are so limiting!

I have stood on platforms and seen cripples who had never walked drag themselves onto the ground, stand up and walk under the power of God. The blind begin to see, deaf-mutes begin to hear, and I can't figure it out. It's beyond my concept, but I know it happens just like I know that when I plant that tomato seed and give it the right temperature and fertilizer and water, it will produce a tomato.

There are things that God has left hidden from us on purpose, and for us to pry into them and to try to understand them is rebellion against Him. If He wants us to learn, He will reveal it to us. I don't mean that we are putting a premium on ignorance; we believe in academic excellence. God didn't give you the ability to think so you could just take up space and time, He wants you to use your abilities under the guidance of the Holy Spirit and with the help, revelation, and illumination of the Holy Spirit.

We realize from Corinthians that are our warfare is not with carnal but with spiritual weapons, to bring every thought into obedience to Christ, to come against every imagination, every reasoning, everything that exalts itself against the knowledge of God. This means that words become important. Words are so important to God that He says not one dot over an "i" or one cross over a "t" will fail; He says He watches over His Word to perform it. It is settled forever in heaven! It is so important to God that even a dot over an "i" will be fulfilled on time. If we are going to understand the meaning of God's Word, we will have to understand the fact that words are exact. That means if we are going to have the mind of Christ, we must learn to allow God to give us His concepts and His words. Our society teaches that alcoholism is a disease, but an alcoholic doesn't walk down a street and come under an invasion of bacteria for which we don't have any antibiotics; it wasn't any viral infection that hit his body because of eating some kind of a banana from a foreign country that made him become an alcoholic. It is not a disease—it is SIN.

Wrong words bring wrong concepts, and *if we are going to have the helmet of salvation we will have to learn to use correct terminology.* It is not always comfortable and is not always easy, but the mind of Christ requires it. The Word of the Lord is so exact that after all of the scrutiny of some of the finest minds in the history of man, they cannot really find a verifiable fault in His Word.

To have the mind of Christ means that our thought life has to be brought into submission to the Lord and to the Spirit of God. It means that we must be open to receive God's thoughts as our thoughts. There is a place in our walk with God where our thoughts are not our own, where they are the thoughts of Christ. Jesus said, "That which I speak unto you, I received a commandment of the Father what I should say and what I should speak. I have not spoken of myself the word; it is the word of the Father" (John 12:49; 14:10). He knew the difference between His thoughts and the thoughts of the Father.

When we walk with God, we find many problems with carnality. There are people who are spiritually zealous but without knowledge, discipline, or maturity in their walk with the Lord who utter their own minds and think it is the mind of Christ. Sometimes you hear some real strange prophecies that people give, and by the time they get through with the prophecy they haven't said anything. If the Lord speaks to you, you have something to say.

There is a place where our thoughts are not our own, but that place comes out of a relationship where we are entering into what we call UNION WITH GOD. That is what John 14 is all about, and as we come into this relationship with maturity we have the mind of Christ, and as we have the mind of Christ, we know what God is saying in a situation.

Discerning the mind of Christ, then, is important in warfare because the enemy sends the darts of his thoughts into your mind, stimulates your carnal nature and creates confusion. The Scripture says that where there is confusion and strife, there is every evil work. That is why when you go to war, it does not matter how many times you were slain in the Spirit, how many three-dimensional technicolor visions you had, how many people have been healed when you prayed or how many times you have seen the devil cast out of someone who was demonized, because WHEN YOU ENTER INTO THE BATTLE YOU WILL NEED THE TRUTH OF GOD'S WORD, AND THE ONLY THING YOU CAN STAND ON IS TRUTH. If you do not know truth is a particular area, then you will stand in a place of confusion. Take any of the controversies in the Body of Christ today: the prosperity teaching, the teaching of shepherding, or the teaching that Christians can be demon possessed. You will find if you get into a circumstance where one of those issues is relevant without knowing the truth, you will be tossed to and fro because you won't have anything solid to stand on, and you will be defeated in war.

I remember a meeting in which the pattern for the workers was very poorly developed. Many people were responding to the altar call to be saved. I was working in that meeting as the chairman of the counselors, and the minister announced they didn't have enough counselors and said that anyone who would like to help counsel should come. When you ask for everything, that is what you get. So everything came, and there was a fourteen-year-old girl with four or five grown men standing over her screaming at the top of their lungs, trying to cast a devil out. When I saw what was happening, I went over and tried to stop them and had to physically pull them away because they would not respond. I told them there was no devil to cast out. I reached down to the girl and asked her why she came to the altar, and she said, "I wanted to receive the Baptism of the Holy Spirit." I talked with her for about three minutes, prayed for her, and she immediately received the Baptism of the Holy Spirit as these ministers and pastors watched, not having the mind of Christ, confused about what was going on and making room for a demonic type of experience. With what they were doing, the confusion that was present released the enemy to come in and start to traumatize that little girl.

If you don't know what is going on, you can't give anyone truth. Here comes a woman who is divorced; you have the divorce/remarriage issue. She doesn't know whether she can get married again. What are you going to give her, *your* opinion? "Well, you are twenty-six years old; you married a guy who turned out to be a creep; he walked out on you and he's living with another woman; you have three kids to raise and you weren't even saved when you married him. You have never been in adultery; you've come to know Christ and you're trying to walk with the Lord." What do you tell her? "No, you've got to abide single all your life or you'll go to hell as an adulterer," or "Yes, you can get remarried." You need to know the truth of God's word or you cannot help that person, and I'll guarantee that any young lady who is in that position will go through demonic attack. The enemy will come to her and rip her to shreds, causing her to feel that if she has any desire for remarriage, she is lost and going to hell, and that if she tries not to remarry, her life is empty and meaningless; because of a little mistake before she was saved she is doomed to a life of emptiness and loneliness. That kind of a person will go through all kinds of torment, and the only thing that will set her free is truth. JESUS SAID, "YOU WILL KNOW THE TRUTH AND THE TRUTH SHALL MAKE YOU FREE."

YOU CANNOT GO TO WAR AND EXPECT TO BE SUCCESSFUL IF YOU DON'T HAVE THE MIND OF CHRIST, IF YOU DON'T KNOW THE TRUTH OF GOD'S WORD! That means that since God provided His Word for us, we should at least be willing to try and find out what it says!

The Scripture shows us that we will have confusion and strife; we won't know where to plant our feet; we won't know what position to resist or what position to support unless we have truth. That is where the helmet of salvation comes in. We must have salvation, we must be born again, and we must come into the mind of Christ.

Part of what is involved in the mind of Christ is your imagination, not just knowledge that you have by facts. We all have to perceive facts in the truth of God's Word, but we have an image-making faculty that has creative power, because as a man thinks, so is he. If you think of yourself in a certain way, that is what you become in your spirit and you will act it out in your life. IF YOU CAN NEVER CONCEIVE OF YOURSELF LAYING HANDS ON THE SICK AND PRAYING THE PRAYER OF FAITH AND SEEING PEOPLE HEALED, IT WILL NEVER HAPPEN IN YOUR LIFE. IF YOU CAN NEVER CONCEIVE OF YOURSELF STANDING IN FULL AND COMPLETE VICTORY WITHOUT A TREMEND-OUS BATTLE RAGING ON THE INSIDE IN THE FACE OF A TEMPTATION THAT YOU ARE STRUGGLING WITH TODAY, YOU WILL NEVER STAND IN VICTORY! As a man thinks in his heart, so is he.

As we come into the mind of Christ and think correctly, we can learn to deal with our fallen nature correctly and see it come under the power of the Cross, releasing us into resurrection life to where we can stand in the place of victory. We can see ourselves in victory in Christ, and that creates vision. Vision is a mental concept, an image, a dream, a desire, and if it is sanctified then you have hope. And these three abide: hope, faith, and love. Hope *always* precedes faith. You have faith in something, and that something is a vision, an image, and when you first see that vision or image and you don't really have faith for it yet, it is a hope-so situation. When you start to press in towards what God has shown you, as your image-making faculty has come into the realm of Christ and you see where God is taking you, as you begin to see Jesus as He is, then you are changed from glory to glory, even into His likeness and image. As you see that image as a hope and there is a difference between what you see and what you are, there is a process by which you are metamorphosed into the image of Christ. So you get your hope-so's into the purposes of God and you go into a process of transformation.

Our image-making faculty is a very important thing to guard in our lives. A woman is married and has two kids in diapers. Her husband is a workaholic. He is working real hard, trying to grow in his career, putting in the extra hours so he can climb the ladder. He comes home and he is tired and doesn't relate to his wife. He is a little irritable because of the pressures of the job; she is a little on edge because she has had screaming kids all day and wants to talk to someone with a higher mentality than a two-year-old, but the husband doesn't particularly want to hear a woman talking about changing diapers because he has other problems. And you have a little situation develop. Because she has nothing to do, she turns on the soap opera or reads some novel or magazine, and the next thing you know she remembers Joe Doe who was her boyfriend in high school and the wonderful times they used to have. She is bored with her married life. She remembers the excitement of Joe Doe and the next thing you know, Joe Doe calls on the phone and says he just happened to be in town and wants to see her. He has made it in this world and is at the top making good money. The wife is in a trap. She did not guard her image-making faculty and allowed the enemy to come in and set her up, and when she bought into the project, he brought by Joe Doe.

We need the helmet of salvation to guard our thoughts, bringing every thought into the captivity and obedience to Christ. What are you doing with your thought life, with your imagination? What do you do when someone close to you hurts you, and you nurse that thing and rehearse it over and over again in your mind? One thing you are doing is heading yourself into depression and ill health from the poisons released in your body because of the bitterness, resentment, and unforgiveness. You are alienating yourself from those around you. You are walking away from God because He said that if you don't forgive, He won't forgive you. You are headed for a fall.

When you go to war, you will find that you get wounded, and you are wounded in the household of your friends. It doesn't hurt me when someone filled with the devil comes up and lays into me, but it does hurt if someone I have been close to, to whom I have opened my innermost being and shared with heart to heart, misuses that kind of intimacy. The breastplate of righteousness comes on to protect our feelings and to keep the right response, which has to do with seeking reconciliation, encountering, admonition, forgiving, and bringing it to the Lord. *If we ever learn anything from Calvary, it is that it costs something to love.*

We must also watch what we do with our words. We must watch what we do with our circumstances and what we are doing with our thought life. That is part of the helmet of salvation, and the enemy knows that if he can get you on any of these kinds of problems, he will render you ineffective. He will probe to find your weak spot; he will set you up and he'll pull the rug or push the domino; whatever it takes.

There is a connection between the helmet of salvation and the sword of the Spirit. THE SWORD OF THE SPIRIT IS A WORD FROM THE LORD, THE RHEMA OF GOD. THAT PERSONAL WORD FROM GOD WILL *NEVER* VIOLATE THE PRINCIPLES OF HIS WRITTEN WORD. IT WILL NEVER SHOW YOU A DIFFERENT ATTITUDE OR DIFFERENT PRIORITIES OR DIFFERENT METHODS THAN WHAT GOD'S WORD SAYS. IT WILL NEVER VIOLATE THE CHARACTER TRAITS OF GOD AS REVEALED IN THE SCRIPTURE. YOU CAN STUDY THE BIBLE ALL YOU WANT AND YOU WILL LEARN GENERAL PRINCIPLES, BUT WHEN YOU GET THROUGH UNDERSTANDING THE PRINCIPLES OF

GOD'S WORD AND OF GUIDANCE AND OF HEARING

HIS VOICE, YOU ARE RELIGIOUS. THEN YOU MUST HAVE REALITY OF RELATIONSHIP WHERE IT IS WORKED OUT IN YOU INDIVIDUALLY, AND THAT TAKES YOU OUT OF RELIGION AND INTO REALITY.

You are going along and you say, "It is wonderful to serve the Lord and give my life to Him; it is His; He is Lord of all that I am, all that I have, and all that I'll ever be." Wonderful. That is a necessary prerequisite, but it is not enough. The next thing you find out is that God has a purpose in this world and He is trying to reach the lost. Not only so, those who are reached He is trying to conform into the image of Christ. How are you going to be a part of His program? Are you going to Rio de Janeiro? Are you going to go to Bombay or Bangkok? Novato? Are you going to be a pastor/evangelist? Are you going to be a local deacon? Someone who works in an industry? Biblically, all those things are correct, but God has a plan for you and it is as unique as you are. That is part of the mind of Christ; that is part of the sword of the Spirit. You need to tie into God's divine purpose for you, and as you do, start walking in it. Many people ask me why I know what is going on and what is coming up next in this church. It is because God has placed me here as pastor. He tells me about things because that is His purpose and I am flowing in that purpose in my life. Not because I have blond hair and blue eyes; not because I have a Ph.D; but because I am in His will.

When you get into God's will and start flowing in it, He will give you the rhema and you will become an integral part of what God is doing in the local church and around the world. Did you know there is no separation? I am vitally a part of what God is doing in Red China because I and my brethren are one. Most Christians don't realize they are a vital part, so they don't do anything. They are what I call dead members; they don't function. But every one of us as Christians have a mandate from God's Word to an entire lost generation in every nation. You may not be called to Red China but there is one thing you can do: you can pray for that country. You can allow God to give you the mind of Christ on how to pray for it. You might be able to give financially to certain individuals. There are all kinds of ways you can participate. How you carry out God's mandate, how you discover it, is hidden in the mind of Christ. That is part of having the helmet of salvation and it comes to you as the rhema, as God speaks to you and begins to unfold it in your life and leads and directs you into His unique purpose for you as an individual. When you hear His voice, you must respond to it, you must embrace it, and walk in it.

Once that Word comes, and it is genuine, and you get hold of it, you can walk through hell on it. You can walk right down to the throneroom and watch the enemy's knees shake together when you have that Word from ;God. I wouldn't say that if I hadn't walked in it. I have gotten hold of the Word of God and I have acted on it and have allowed my life to hang on whether God meant what He said or not, and I have found Him to be faithful and true, to mean exactly what He has said.

What is it that God is speaking to you about? Are you getting His vision? Are you finding out what God has? Are you beginning to build this particular element of armour, the mind of Christ? The mind of Christ doesn't mean that you don't think about dirty thoughts; you have been brainwashed—washed with the Blood. *Being renewed by the Spirit means that you come into a knowledge of God's will,* not just in the ethereal, in the abstract, or in generalities, but *in the specific and particular as related to you and how you relate to it.* You may have started with the abstract ("God doesn't want me to smoke or chew or run with those who do"), and you get that changed in your life, but you need more. If that is all you get, you will find yourself susceptible to the attack of the enemy and you are going to say, "My life is empty, I don't have any meaning or fulfillment. I want to do something for God but I don't know what it is. What is wrong with me?" You need to get hold of the mind of Christ. Get out of that square hole as a round peg and find the round hole that God has for you. Find out what He has in your life!

Remember that although many are called, few are chosen and although He may call you to a placement, it does not mean that you are ready to walk in that placement. *There is a difference between the calling and the choosing.* If you apply for a position with a company, there will be many who are called and interviewed, and there will be a few who are chosen to fill the slots. Why are they chosen? Because they *qualify.* If you ever want to go on with God, put that word in bold type and neon lights in your Spirit. QUALIFY.

Some maybe never knew that God called them; others may know what God has called them to but they are not ready. Getting the mind of Christ means that not only do you find out what your place is, you qualify for it by being READY. You know what you need to know in order to do what God has asked you to do. You are prepared in your spirit; you are prepared in your priorities; you are prepared in your relationships; you are prepared in your loyalties, knowledge, skills, and abilities. Then you qualify. Why do you think Jesus spent three and one half years preparing the apostles?

When I think of the helmet of salvation, these are the kinds of thoughts that go through my mind. I know that when I go to war, I have to be ready. When you stand on a platform with 100,000 people expecting to see the miracle power of God and there is another group who has come to storm the platform and start a riot and take your life, and there is another group who are skeptics, and the nationals are scared to death, you have to know that you are qualified. You wouldn't dare to presume to step into that kind of situation out of your mind. You need to know what is going on. Nothing should come down as a surprise, you should be prepared, you should have learned about it, God should have taught you about it and you should know how to respond and deal with it.

Not only should you have knowledge about it, you should have had some preliminary experience to begin to develop those processes in your life SO THAT WHEN THE ENEMY ATTACKS, YOU STAND SOLID, YOU STAND IN FAITH, YOU STAND UNWAVERING, YOU STAND BOLD AND CONFIDENT. You don't find that you are thrown around. You are shod with the gospel of peace; you are girded with the preparation of the gospel; you have the breastplate of righteousness, the helmet of salvation, the shield of faith, and the sword of the Spirit, and when the enemy attacks and you are moving in God's purpose, you can take the sword of the Spirit and slay the enemy and come home with the victory! And if you are really out on the front line doing something for God without walking with the qualifiers in your life, you won't come home with any victory but you will come home bruised, scarred, beaten, wounded, and terribly ashamed.

War is an ugly word. Never make something pleasant out of it. War is tragedy. When I first started to go on the mission field on front lines of unreached peoples and unreached cities where 90 percent had never heard the name of Jesus, I had a kind of a glorification in my mind. I thought of how wonderful it was to see the victories and the glory of God, the healings and the salvation, the churches starting out of the crusades. But as I got into it, I found out what the other two-thirds of the iceberg were like. I found out what it is like under the hand of God to be ground to powder, to have everything that I had ever received from the Lord challenged and to have it crushed and to die a thousand deaths every day. How we need the helmet of salvation in order to stand!

> Lord, I'm asking that You would just work to bring every imagination, every vision, every concept into alignment with your divine intent and purpose. Father, that there will be hope and vision created to produce discipline and effort, to bring forth hope and faith and life transformation. Father, the wrong patterns, the rehearsals of injury and hurt, the fantasy and escapism, cause them to be dealt with by your

Spirit and replaced with your provision and your truth. Lord, You said that if we would diligently seek You, You would reward us. If we would draw near to You, You would draw near to us. I am believing You, Lord, according to the promise of your Word that if any two would agree it would be given of your Father. I agree with these brethren that your purpose, your intent, your will, will begin to be manifest to them as they seek You earnestly in prayer and obedience. I believe You for it, Jesus. Amen.

12

The Sword of the Spirit

> ... and the sword of the Spirit, which is the word of
> God. Eph. 6:17

The sword of the Spirit is God's own utterance given to us in
His written Word inspired and revealed to us by the Spirit, and it
is to be used by the Spirit of God in us to sanctify, to cleanse, and
to work a work in warfare. There is both confusion and vital truth
in this area today. The enemy likes to muddy the waters so we
miss the truth that will set us free and make us effective.

Throughout the Scripture I am aware of two major offensive
weapons in warfare: one of them is the sword of the Spirit, the
rhema of God, and the other is a proper understanding and
function of praise and worship in our lives, and they are vitally
related. If we do not understand them, then we have only
defensive measures and we cannot do very well in war. That
would be Vietnam revisited. Our people there were being asked to
lay down their lives without striking back at the enemy. We could
defend ourselves but we could never cross the demilitarized zone
and make a good strike at the enemy and put him down once and
for all. We had to stand in a place of exposure without wiping out
the enemy, and that is the position in which we would be in
spiritual warfare. Jesus said, "Whatever you do, do heartily as
unto the Lord." WHEN YOU GO TO WAR AGAINST THE
ENEMY, YOU CANNOT GIVE HIM ANY GROUND. HE
WHO HESITATES WILL GIVE THE ADVANTAGE TO
THE ENEMY, and if you know the kind of enemy we are
battling spiritually, you will recognize that we have absolutely no
room to show him mercy because he will never show us any
mercy!

I love the picture of Elisha the prophet on his death bed. The
king of Israel, Joash, came and asked for advice. The Word of the
Lord came to the prophet and he took an arrow from a quiver
and shot it out the window. He asked the king to take the quiver
of arrows and to beat it on the ground, and because the king was
the kind of man that he was, he lightly tapped it on the ground
three times. The Scripture says that the prophet of God was
angry; he said, "Thou shouldest have smitten five or six times;
then hadst thou smitten Syria till thou hadst consumed it:
whereas now thou shalt smite Syria but thrice" (2 Kings 13:19).
So it is in spiritual warfare. The kind of enemy you and I battle in
the Spirit is the one that when you get him down, you should
continue to smite him until there is no possibility of recovery. You

must keep pressing on, and if you hesitate you will give him the advantage; he will not hesitate against you.

When we go to spiritual war, we need to use our offensive weapons; we will not do very well in the battle without them. With the sword of the Spirit you can put the enemy to rest, you can destroy him and take the victory.

Each time temptation came to Jesus in the wilderness, He said, "It is written" and used the Word of God as a sword, and He stood in victory. In the middle of your battle, none of your wonderful experiences in the Spirit will be of value to you. You must lay hold of the rhema of God, and you can cleave to it with your spiritual hands, you can walk into the midst of the battle with the enemy and wield that sword and take the victory even in the throneroom of hell! But without it, all you can do is fortify your defenses. If you do not have a good offense, defeat is imminent. Therefore, it is vital to know what the sword of the Spirit is.

The Scripture says that the sword of the Spirit is the rhema of God. The word "rhema" has been used and defined by some to be the word that is spoken, but that is not biblical. In the Greek language in which the New Testament was written, we have two basic words that are translated "word" in English—*logos* and *rhema.* They are two different things. The Gospel of John begins, "In the beginning was the *logos,* and the *logos* was with God and the *logos* was God, and the *logos* became flesh and dwelt among us." The references to the written Word are always logos. The logos, then, is Christ in His fullness.

In the Book of Luke, the angel of the Lord had come to Mary and told her she was going to conceive by the Holy Spirit and the holy thing that would be born by her would be the Messiah. Her response to that was:

> Behold the handmaid of the Lord; be it unto me according to thy *rhema.* And the angel departed from her. Luke 1:38

Rhema here was a word that God sent through His messenger to Mary personally. There is no way you can claim that as your word. There isn't another woman who will ever walk the face of the earth who will conceive of the Holy Spirit and have a physical child born who is the Christ. That was a *personal* word from God to Mary. *It revealed something of the purpose of God.* It revealed something of the character of God, and it was extremely personal, not universal.

In Luke 2 the baby Jesus was taken into the temple to be dedicated to the Lord, and there was a prophet of God who picked Jesus up and gave thanks to God. He then said, "Lord, now lettest thou thy servant depart in peace, according to thy *rhema:* For mine eyes have seen thy salvation, Which thou hast prepared before the face of all people" (Luke 2:29-31). The promise of God to this man was that he was not going to die until he saw the salvation of God. As this prophet of God was standing in the temple the day that Mary and Joseph brought Jesus in, he walked over, held Him up and by the revelation of the Spirit knew who this baby Jesus was. *The rhema had given him peace* that he would not die until he saw the Messiah.

Annas and Caiaphas being the high priests, the *rhema* of God came unto John the son of Zacharias in the wilderness. And he came into all the country about Jordan, preaching the baptism of repentance for the remission of sins. Luke 3:2, 3

As the greatest prophet of the Old Testament, according to Jesus, John the Baptist came forth with the Word of the Lord for the people. God gave it to him; it was a rhema of God.

In Luke 5 Peter had been told by Jesus to launch his boat and to drop his nets into the water and he would get some fish. Peter did not believe it, saying,

Master, we have toiled all the night, and have taken nothing; nevertheless at thy *rhema* I will let down the net. Luke 5:5

The catch was so great it broke the net. That word to go out and let down his net to catch fish was not to every fisherman who would ever go out on the Sea of Galilee. They could not look at that verse, take their boats and say, "I claim your word, Lord," and get a drought of fish. *It was a personal word of God to Peter at a specific moment in time; it was his and his alone. That is the character and nature of the rhema of God.* To use it in any other context, then, is to take it out of the context of the Word.

As I began to speak, the Holy Spirit fell on them, as on us at the beginning. Then remembered I the *rhema* of the Lord, how that he said, John indeed baptized with water; but ye shall be baptized with the Holy Ghost. Acts 11:15, 16

And the second time the cock crew. And Peter called to mind the *rhema* that Jesus said unto him, Before the cock crow twice, thou shalt deny me thrice. Mark 14:72

Peter remembered the *rhema* of the Lord. Understanding its usage, *we need to take a look at how it is applied.*

There are things that God speaks to us individually as we learn to walk with Him, and those things will never violate the logos, or they are not a rhema. *If it violates the revelation of God, His character, His motivation, His purposes, His ways, and His written Word, then it is not from God.* But if it meets those standards, that Word from God has tremendous potential. *The rhema brings faith.*

> Faith cometh by hearing, and hearing by the *rhema* of God. Rom. 10:17

You cannot have faith in that which you do not know is God's will. If you are sick and need healing, it is hard to believe for healing and receive it if you are not sure that it is God's will to heal you. But if the Word of the Lord comes to you by the Spirit of God and He says, "You are healed, receive it," and you accept it, that rhema of God produces faith and you receive your healing. If you are seeking God in prayer and He speaks to you in your spirit and says, "I want you to yield your life unto Me for a lifetime of service for the Kingdom," and you are not sure it is really the Lord, ask God to confirm it to you. The next thing you know some traveling evangelist comes through or your pastor comes by who doesn't know what you are praying about, and in the course of conversation he says, "I believe God has a special call to the ministry on your life." Maybe you turn around and go to another meeting and the Word of the Lord comes forth and says, "Why are you delaying? Why do you halt? Do not pull back in unbelief but move forward in the word that I have spoken unto you, and I will do great and mighty things in your life!"

There are confirmations. There are safety factors to judge a word to be sure that it is a rhema of God, but when you determine it to be so, it produces faith. What else does the rhema of God produce? Jesus said,

> It is written, Man shall not live by bread alone, but by every *rhema* that proceedeth out of the mouth of God. Matt. 4:4

The rhema not only produces faith, it produces life. You need something to live by spiritually. That which will sustain you is to live by every rhema that proceeds out of the mouth of God. When God speaks to you, how do you eat of His Word? As bread sustains your body, the Word sustains your spirit. You embrace the rhema to do it, to walk in it; you receive it, you act on it, you allow your life to hang on God's faithfulness to His Word.

> [Jesus] being the brightness of his glory, and the express image of his person, and upholding all things by the *rhema* of his power. Heb. 1:3

All things are upheld by the rhema of Jesus' power. The chair you are sitting on, the carpet you walk on, *all things* are upheld, all things by Him consist, by the rhema of His power! The rhema carries with it creative power; it carries with it the ability to bring faith; faith brings into manifestation the thing hoped for, it brings it to life. What happened when you got saved? You knelt at the foot of Calvary, where you said, "Jesus, forgive me of my sin, cleanse me from all unrighteousness, come into my heart, give me the miracle of the new birth." And in your spirit you heard the voice of God as His rhema came unto you in one form or another saying, "You are forgiven" or "I receive you. You are my child." And with that Word came faith to accept the miracle of salvation, and that Word began to cause something to take place. You began to understand that as Christ was made sin for us, you were made the righteousness of God in Him. When God spoke this to your spirit, you were in the midst of the filthiness of sin and of rebellion and full of all kinds of uncleanness, but the power of that Word in your spirit started changing your motivations, perceptions, values, desires, and goals, and you began to be transformed. And you are still in the process of responding to that one rhema that is causing you to be changed from glory to glory into His likeness and image! *The end of that rhema is that you will be found as He is.*

Application: Jesus came to the blind man and said, "Be thou made whole." That was a personal word from the Lord. The power of that word was that he was healed immediately. Ten lepers came to the Lord and He touched them and said, "Be clean," and the power of that personal word from the Lord was that they were cleansed from their leprosy. He came to the grave of Lazarus and said, "Lazarus, come forth!" and the power of that personal word from the Lord was the power to raise him from the dead. It was a fantastic miracle of healing!

Husbands, love your wives, even as Christ loved the church, and gave himself for it; That he might sanctify and cleanse it with the washing of water by the *rhema,* That he might present it to himself a glorious church, not having spot, or wrinkle, or any such thing; but that it should be holy and without blemish. Eph. 5:25-27

The rhema of God has cleansing, sanctifying power. When God speaks to our spirit and we receive the Word, it cleanses and sanctifies us and the will of God is revealed, illuminated, manifest.

We came back to this phrase: "And take the sword of the spirit which is the rhema of God." Many people get confused in their walk with God because all they have is a method, and they think that the method is a formula: "Well, just confess it. I'm healed, I'm healed, I'm healed, I'm healed. . . ." That doesn't make you healed. Another person says, "I don't have a fever. My temperature is 105 but I don't have a fever. Don't confess you have a fever; it'll make you sick." The Scripture says to call the elders of the church and ask for prayer to be healed according to God's Word.

There are all kinds of methods and approaches, but the walk with God that is built on methods is that which is not *with* God, it is *for* God; it is a walk where we put ourselves as the sovereign and try to have God be our head butler to run at our beck and call. "God I am going to initiate what I want by my confession or my method and You bless it." Sometimes it is shocking to people to realize that God is the Sovereign and we are His servants! *The rhema of God, when properly understood, keeps us in the place of servant before the Master, because He initiates; He speaks the word to us,* and if He doesn't speak the word to us, we don't have a word and all we can do is spin our wheels in exercises of futility and vanity. BUT WHEN YOU GET THE RHEMA OF GOD, IT PRODUCES FAITH; IT PRODUCES LIFE; IT PRODUCES CLEANSING; IT PRODUCES CREATIVE POWER; IT WALKS THROUGH HELL AND THE POWERS OF DARKNESS BOW BEFORE IT!

This means you must have a relationship with God. You don't get a rhema from God if you are just any Tom, Dick, and Harry walking down the street; He doesn't speak to just everybody. God is so different than we are. If we have a kingdom we would want the whole world to know about it and we would just stick it right there in the sky and everyone would look up and see it. God hid His Kingdom, and not everyone can see it. Jesus said, "Except a man be born of the kingdom of God, or born of the Spirit, he cannot see the kingdom of heaven, nor can he enter into it." So all the lost people out there are blinded to the realm of the Kingdom of God, and they operate on different principles. GOD HAS CHOSEN TO HIDE HIS KINGDOM AND IF WE ARE GOING TO SEE IT, IT IS BECAUSE GOD CHOOSES TO REVEAL IT TO US. *And when you have a rhema from God, there is something of the will of God that is revealed in it, something of the purpose and intent, nature and character of God.*

When God speaks, things happen. He says, "Let there be light," and there is light; "Lazarus, come forth," and he came forth; "Be clean," and leprosy disappears. There is power in His word and when He speaks, He usually doesn't tell you something as simple as "Don't buy Del Monte tuna, buy Bumble Bee tuna." Some people say God is always talking to them, telling them to get up at 9:08 and 50 seconds and what bread to buy. They are just bound up in the vanity of their own minds. If God was telling them anything, He would have something to say! As one dear brother has said, GOD IS AT LEAST INTELLIGENT!!

I am walking in the things that God has spoken to my life and to my spirit fourteen years ago. I am walking on the Word that God spoke to me, and I am still drawing life from it!

How does God speak? Hebrews 11:6 says, "He that cometh to God must believe that he is, and that he is a rewarder of them that diligently seek him." If you are going to go to war you will need the rhema of God or you won't have a sword to strike the enemy with. That means you will have to lay hold of God, because THE METHOD IS THE PERSON OF JESUS CHRIST. WITH HIM NOTHING IS IMPOSSIBLE, AND IN HIS PRESENCE IS THE FULLNESS OF JOY, AT HIS RIGHT HAND THERE ARE PLEASURES FOREVER MORE. THE NAME OF THE LORD IS A STRONG TOWER AND THE RIGHTEOUS RUNS IN TO IT AND IS SAFE. **HE IS YOUR DEFENSE. HE IS YOUR REWARD. HE IS YOUR REFUGE. HE IS YOUR SAVIOUR. HE IS YOUR MIGHTY LION OF THE TRIBE OF JUDAH. HE IS YOUR CONQUERING KING. HE IS YOUR HIGH PRIEST. HE IS THE ONE WHO SUCCORS AND STRENGTHENS YOU. HE IS ALL THAT YOU NEED!** YOU HAVE TO LAY HOLD OF HIM, and that begins by believing that God is. You also must believe that He is the rewarder of those who diligently seek Him. Jesus' Word tells us, "Draw near to me and I will draw near unto you."

Some people do not know how to lay hold of God; others just don't want to pay the price. Many times people will in need come for counseling. They can be shown direction, but they have to lay hold of God for themselves. When they need a spiritual breakthrough, no one else can give it to them; only Jesus can do it.

How badly do you want to hear from God? "Well, I fasted and prayed four hours every day for three whole days, but God didn't speak to me." Oh? Maybe He did speak to you. While you were fasting and praying, God maybe said, "Before we can deal with that, you need to be reconciled with so-and-so, and that little habit there in your life has to go. Are you willing to surrender it to me? Or are you going to put in your heels and bow your neck?" When I need to hear from God, He always gets mileage from it. *He never just gives me that Word I need; He always gets something from me.* I'm grateful He is like that because there are many things in my heart that I cling to because of the stubbornness of my sin nature. When I get stubborn like that and God wants something, He allows a circumstance to come when I need to hear from Him, when I need a breakthrough, and as I press in to get it, He holds it out there like a carrot and says, "You see that in your life? I want that, and I want it right now. You can't have the carrot until you give Me what is in your heart." I give it to Him, and the carrot comes—the provision, the breakthrough, the Word, and it is always related to a dimension of surrender from me. *You cannot walk in the anointing and blessing of God today without walking in a greater walk of righteousness and holiness than you did yesterday.*

If you want a genuine rhema from God, then when He begins to put His finger on those things in your life, let go and give them to Him. In Luke 4, as Jesus overcame the test of His spirit, soul, and body by the enemy, He returned in the power of the Spirit. The rhema sanctifies and cleanses, and we must allow the sanctifying and cleansing process to come into our lives to have the power of the Spirit. And what is cleansing but removal? Go out and work on your car and get your hands full of grease and oil. Cleansing is the removal of that oil, grease, and filth. As the rhema comes, it is always with cleansing and sanctifying. Unless we are willing to receive that, we will not receive the genuine rhema from God.

You will not win the spiritual battle without that word from God. One day David is sitting and God says, "Go get them!" The next day, the Lord says, "No, you wait until you hear the rustling in the mulberry trees." What He does today is not necessarily the way He's going to do it tomorrow. You must lay hold of His person and you need to receive a Word from God. It isn't opening the prayer book for the sermon this week. It is laying hold of God and what He is saying today. You can take the Word from the Lord and embrace it, and it will take you to total and complete victory; you can count on it.

I keep going back to Poona as an illustration because it is such a beautiful one. Before the meetings, I spend the afternoon shut in before the Lord in intercession and I don't like to have conversation with anyone. I have enough going on in the spiritual battle against the enemy and my own flesh and keeping the mind of Christ to have to battle someone else's thoughts. I have to be an open channel for what God is going to do. It is a lonely time, but I must wait in that place before God in order to be prepared to be used in these dimensions. So in waiting before the Lord a couple of hours before the Poona meeting, someone knocked on the door and said the police commissioner wanted me in his office, that the crusade chairman had a crisis and left town. Down I went to the commissioner's office and heard the threat of violence. I had to know what God was saying; I couldn't walk into that circumstance in my own mind. I told the police commissioner there was not going to be any riot. The crowds were peaceful; the accusations were not true. I told him we were not interested in responding to the rumors of liars; we wanted to respond to truth, and the truth was what was at issue there. I told him he could go and examine the truth because it would stand up under investigation. I had a Word from the Lord to my heart: "I will bring peace; the meeting will not be closed." I stood in boldness because I had that word from God. The rhema brought peace; it brought faith; it cleansed my own heart; it brought life; and in the midst of it all we stood on that Word and God gave us a great victory.

Father, as we would seek to be effective soldiers in the Spirit, teach us to covet that Word from You, Lord, that we would come to the place where we are able to hear from You. Lord, You are not a respecter of persons, but You are a rewarder of those that diligently seek you. Confirm your Word with signs following in the lives of those who draw near to You. For Jesus' sake, Amen.

13

Prayer

Praying always with all prayer and supplication in the
Spirit, and watching thereunto with all perseverance
and supplication for all saints. Eph. 6:18

Prayer is the powerhouse, the dynamo, the generator, the
spiritual nuclear power plant, the animation behind all of the
armour of God in its operation. UNTIL YOU PRAY,
NOTHING HAPPENS.

Prayer is difficult, especially when you get into the kind of
prayer that is involved in warfare. It helps when you have
corporate prayer, but many times you have to stand alone, and
that is difficult. There is loneliness. There are things that draw
you aside and want to grab your attention that seem to be more
expedient but in fact are not. *Praying in the Spirit is very
important.* It says in Ephesians 6:18, "Praying always with all
prayer and supplication in the Spirit." What does it mean to pray
in the Spirit? Certainly, it does not mean to pray in the natural
man, or the flesh. Galatians says, "If you walk in the Spirit you
will not fulfill the lust of the flesh." Fleshly prayer will accomplish
nothing; you need to get into the Spirit.

Often much of your time in prayer is drawing you out of self,
out of Adam and flesh, and into the Spirit so you can begin to
pray. The more adept you get at that, the easier it is to get into
effective prayer.

So at the very least we must recognize that to pray in the Spirit
must mean that we need to get out of self and into the life flow of
the Spirit of God. This means that we have to begin to pray with
the mind of Christ. We must come to the place where we have
that sword of the Spirit, the rhema of God, so we see from God's
perception what is happening, what to pray for, what to do in that
prayer battle. *Then* you begin to pray. *You must learn to pray out
of the mind of the Spirit.* There is a flow of divine life that brings
with it several things. First, you come into a place where you are
literally with the mind of Christ, visualizing or conceptualizing in
your own mentality what is taking place in the battle manifest in
the Spirit during your prayer. You will recognize in your
intercession certain kinds of spirits of the enemy that are resisting
the purpose of God. As you do, you learn how to deal with those
spirits; you use your authority in Christ against them. You walk
in the power of the Word, the rhema that God has given you to
see them bound and brought down.

Second, while you are praying you discover that you need a supernatural animation of your will. *Your will comes to a place where it is under the influence of the Spirit of Almighty God. You find yourself with commitments in prayer that go far beyond what you would ever find in the natural.* This often is the result of beginning to feel what God feels. *You begin to sense what God senses.* When you get into deep intercession, there will be times when your body will travail and sob and you will have involuntary muscle contractions just like a woman does when she is bringing birth to a child. *THERE IS A DEPTH OF PATHOS THAT COMES INTO YOUR SPIRIT, A SENSE OF FEELING AND EMPATHY, A SENSE OF AWARENESS OF THE LOVE OF GOD, THE DESIRE, FORCE, PAIN AND AGONY OF SUFFERING AND SIN AND DARKNESS THAT COMES FROM A SUPERNATURAL SENSE OF THE SPIRIT WHICH MOTIVATES AND PRESSES YOU.* The love of God constrains and presses us as we enter into genuine intercession, and as you do you will find that it has physiological reactions in your body. You can turn them off, but you cannot turn them on. You can resist it, although it will still churn inside and you will have the reaction of grieving the Spirit. Only as the Spirit of God supernaturally burdens you and you get into the Spirit do you find that kind of depth in prayer. This is what it means to really pray in the Spirit.

I remember the first time my wife was with me in India. We were flying from Bombay to Southern India and she was praying for the upcoming meeting and ministers institute. As she was interceding, she suddenly broke into tears and felt a tremendous depth of what God felt for India. It was so overwhelming that she said, "God, turn it off." Have you ever been in the place where you feel you can't take any more? This is what it means to get into the Spirit when you pray. YOU ARE PRESSED BEYOND YOUR OWN CONCERNS, DESIRES, AND AMBITIONS, AND YOU BECOME CONSUMED BY THE SPIRIT OF GOD.

> What is it then? I will pray with the spirit, and I will pray with the understanding also: I will sing with the spirit, and I will sing with the understanding also. 1 Cor. 14:15

The gifts and the operation of the Spirit are spoken of in chapters 12, 13, and 14, so we understand that what Paul means in this passage is praying in tongues. Part of praying in the Spirit is praying in tongues until a direction or rhema comes to your mind as you have the mind of Christ in the area for which you are interceding. When that word or direction comes, you can articulate very specifically that for which you have been interceding in your Spirit and a sense of power is released. When you have really entered into prayer, you can sense when the articulation is right on. You know when you have the word of life and what you are articulating is the mind of the Spirit and when it isn't.

Likewise the Spirit also helpeth our infirmities: for we know not what we should pray for as we ought. but the Spirit itself maketh intercession for us with groanings which cannot be uttered. And he that searcheth the hearts knoweth what is the mind of the Spirit, because he maketh intercession for the saints according to the will of God. Rom. 8:26, 27

Although we are not able to articulate the burden of the Spirit of God in our spirit, we allow the Spirit to be a channel through which He intercedes for and through us. While that is taking place, many times it brings you to a place where you perceive and understand what the spirit is that you are battling; you sense what it is that God is wanting to bring into manifestation and you are able to articulate it with your understanding, which releases the power of God.

If this seems strange to you, I challenge you to cultivate your prayer life. I found this kind of experience in intercession in my first couple of months as a Christian. You don't have to be old in Christ; all you have to do is open yourself up and let the Spirit of God in. As you mature, you will better understand this manifestation of God's Spirit; you will be better able to yield to it and to make yourself available to it, and you can flow with it more easily.

When you intercede and really lay hold of God, it consumes you. The highest calling in ministry that anyone can have is not as an apostle, a prophet of God, a great pastor of a wonderful church, an evangelist or a teacher of the Word. The highest calling of any ministry position in the Body of Christ is to be called to one of intercession. It is a hidden ministry because it is a closet ministry. You will not get recognition from this world; you will not find the people of God patting you on the back; many won't even recognize your ministry. But our Heavenly Father who looks upon the hearts of all men places a great value on the ministry of intercession. How do we know that? In Ezekiel God wanted to withhold judgment from Israel.

And I sought for a man among them, that should make up the hedge, and stand in the gap before me for the land, that I should not destroy it: but I found none. Therefore have I poured out mine indignation upon them; I have consumed them with the fire of my wrath: their own way have I recompensed upon their heads, saith the Lord God. Ezek. 22:30, 31

He said, "I looked for a man that I might withhold judgment." Why? Because God has limited Himself to manifest through His people. He has chosen us as His instruments, and if we will not, He will not. He wanted to pardon Israel and in order to do that, He needed just one man who would fill the gap as an intercessor and because He did not find one, judgment came.

What is an intercessor? He is by definition *one who takes the place of another*. The greatest act of intercession in the Scripture is when Jesus took our place on the Cross of Calvary and received the judgment in His body that was ours, that we might have the blessing that was His. *Until your heart is brought to a place where you are willing in the Spirit to stand between and take whatever the problem is upon your own life, you have not interceded.* You may have requested, you may have brought supplication, but you have not interceded until you have stood in the gap between judgment, the enemy, or the problem, and the individual. It takes a great depth and capacity of Spirit, one we don't have in ourselves. Only Christ has that kind of capacity. It literally is laying down your life for another, and only as the love of God is shed abroad in your spirit by the Holy Spirit are you ever constrained to the point that you can truly intercede.

Another picture of an intercessor is Moses. He stood before God when He was going to wipe out the nation of Israel in judgment because of the idolatry of the golden calf. Moses said, "If you will not pardon them, Lord, blot my name out of the book that thou hast written," and God pardoned Israel. Why? He saw something of Himself in Moses.

The Apostle Paul had the same Spirit when he said in Romans, "I could wish myself accursed for my brethren's sake that they would be saved." It is the Spirit of Christ. When you go to warfare, INTERCESSION MUST BE AT THE ROOTS. IT IS THE DYNAMO, THE ENERGIZER through which all of these other things we have looked at in this study are able to operate.

You say, how can I intercede when I have this job and all of these responsibilities? I recommend a wonderful book called *Rees Howells—Intercessor* by Norman Grubb. Howells was a coal miner who at times was called by God to fast and intercede. He did hard physical labor but fasted and did his job. God wanted to teach him humility and so he had to take his hat off and was embarrassed about it. There are some things that God may ask of you that may seem a little foolish but they will be means by which God tests your willingness to obey, to walk with Him, to believe Him, and to be dependent upon Him. The first person Howells interceded for to be healed died. God showed Howells

He wanted him to know it wasn't any method, it was going to be by Him. As he learned who he was as a channel of God, he entered into intercession and time after time, God intervened until, during World War II, God in prayer was sharing with him the movements of the Nazi forces against the Allies. Before they ever happened, Howells knew about them, interceded, prayed through, saw the enemy bound, and the Allied forces would win. His dimension in intercessory prayer was so phenomenal that it was affecting the entire world.

You are not just a nobody! Maybe you can't go to India or Africa or China, but in the Spirit you can go to every country in this world as an intercessor. As Paul said, "I was absent from the body but I was present in Spirit." You can discern, you can understand, *you can intercede, and you can release the power of God to change a situation as an intercessor! There is no distance with God in prayer because God is everywhere present. You can affect the entire world through a ministry of intercession.*

If you are going to be a warrior in the Spirit, you will have to be an intercessor in a measure and with our mandate to reach a lost world, you must know that mandate was not only for the twelve disciples. THE MANDATE IS FROM GOD FOR YOU TO TOUCH EVERY NATION IN THE WORLD FOR THE GOSPEL OF JESUS CHRIST. You can travel to every nation in the world by the Spirit through intercession and finances, and by making your efforts, work, and job count today as you touch the lost people around you. By being obedient and faithful in those three realms, praying, finance, witness in your area, you can touch every country in this world in your generation for Jesus Christ. And it is not a matter of choice. God has given you a mandate to do it. I have seen how the intercession of a handful of people in two or three churches brought a great victory for a huge city in India and how it cast out the darkness and became a national and international news event. God wants you to know that there is power in your prayer life.

Prayer isn't something you can teach people how to do. It boils out of your heart because you have gotten in the Spirit and have allowed Him to flow. You have allowed Him to burden you in order to permit you to see with His mind and He is pressing you in the Spirit. But there is something we can do to help ourselves, and that is worship. You don't know how to pray; you can't seem to get in the Spirit to pray; you are praying in tongues and it is just as dry as cotton. *The key to praying in the Spirit is His presence*, and the Scripture tells us that He inhabits the praises of His people. *God has an atmosphere*, and in the Scripture, wherever you see God manifested in the heavenly realm, it is in *an atmosphere of praise and worship*. When Jesus came into Jerusalem and they were all praising Him, the Pharisees and the Sadducees said, "You can't have these people praising You like this. Tell them to be quiet." And He said, "If they didn't praise me, the rocks would cry out," because He was the manifest presence of God and wherever He went He lived in an atmosphere of praise and worship. You and I live in an atmosphere: carbon dioxide, hydrogen, oxygen, pollution. Fish live in an atmosphere, some in fresh water, some in salt water. God lives in an atmosphere of praise and worship from His creation. The Scripture tells us that we come into His gates with praise and into His courts with thanksgiving.

Praise is different than worship. It is always centered around what God does, while worship is centered around who God is; His person as opposed to His actions.

Whoso offereth praise glorifieth me: and to him that ordereth his conversation aright will I show the salvation of God. Ps. 50:23

The Hebrew reads:

Whoso offers praise glorifies me: and I will open up a way before him that I can show forth my victory.

There are many biblical examples of that. The water coming out of the rock is just like coming out of that hard place when you find the stream of living water, and that is when the Amalekites, a type of the flesh, always show up to try to cause damage. They want to shut down the life flow. The flesh wants the attention, and when Christ is in the center it can't stand it! The natural man will always seek to gether the attention away from God.

The Amalekites showed up for a battle with Israel. The Israelites interceded and prayed, and Moses' hands were lifted up in an act of surrender and worship. They prevailed in the battle but when Moses' hands would fall down, the Amalekites would win (Exodus 17). The key was the intercessory worship of Moses.

In 2 Kings 3:15, you have the king of Israel who asked for a word from the Lord. They called the prophet Elisha, who asked for a minstrel. When the minstrel played, the hand of the Lord came upon Elisha. When he began to worship and release the life flow of God, then God spoke to him and he prophesied the Word of the Lord to the king of Israel.

As the fining pot for silver, and the furnace for gold; so is a man to his praise. Prov. 27:21

As you worship and praise, there is a motivation and purification that comes into your heart, because you cannot genuinely worship God without a heart of love towards Him.

173

You might praise Him, but worship is an expression of love.

Let the high praises of God be in their mouth, and a two edged sword in their hand. Ps. 149:6

What is the two-edged sword? The rhema of God. Where do you get that rhema? He speaks to you. You have to get into God's presence, so you worship and you praise, you come into His presence and He gives you the rhema. What for?

To execute vengeance upon the heathen, and punishments upon the people; To bind their kings with chains, and their nobles with fetters of iron. Ps. 149:7, 8

We wrestle not against flesh and blood, the Scripture tells us, but against principalities and powers. What do the kings and nobles represent in a heathen country? *A certain principality that is ruled by darkness.* It is to execute upon them the judgment written, that is THE POWER OF GOD TO BIND THE WORK OF THE ENEMY, TO SEE THE MANIFESTATION OF GOD'S WILL AMONGST THOSE PEOPLE. And this honor have all his saints (Ps. 149:9).

Looking at Acts 16, you see the story of Paul and Silas in jail after being beaten and put in stocks. At about midnight they were having a great worship service, singing praises unto God. The presence of God came and sent an earthquake that caused all the stocks to be broken and they were set free. No prayer, just worship and praise.

In 2 Chronicles 20 we have the story of Jehoshaphat as the Ammonites and the Moabites came against him, a type of demon force. As they went out to battle and Jehoshaphat sought God, He said, "Send out the praisers." They just marched out there singing and praising unto the Lord, and the enemy came and was slain by angelic forces because God supernaturally intervened. Can you see it now? We find ourselves back in the Vietnam War and the president says, "What we'll do is get all the people of God out there with their timbrels, trumpets, and guitars and they'll go out there and sing praises to God and march right towards China!" That is warfare!

I think that the best defense oftentimes is a good offense. In a football game, the team that has the ball in possession two-thirds of the game is most likely the one that wins. A good thing to do in warfare is to have the ball. The only way to get ahead is to go straight forward; you have your power pack of the rhema of God, the sword of the Spirit and the high praises of God in your mouth, and you slay the enemy.

We have the authority that whatsoever we bind on earth will be bound in heaven, and whatsoever we loose on earth will be loosed in heaven. We find this in Matthew where Jesus said, "Upon this rock I will build my church and the gates of hell shall not prevail against it. I give you the keys of the kingdom." Those keys are "whatsoever you bind on earth is bound in heaven and whatsoever you loose on earth is loosed in heaven." So through the authority that you have in Jesus Christ, with the high praises and rhema of God, you go forth and wield that sword and use the shield of faith against the darts of the enemy, the enemy turns tail and runs and you jab him real good with the sword and take the victory!

In our crusades in third world countries I tell my assistant to give the nationals one song that they like and to have them sing it over and over again, and to get as many people in the crowd as possible to learn it. That is a battle plan! We aren't out there doing an exercise in futility, or guessing what we are doing. We *know*. The Word of God tells us that this is a weapon of warfare and we release the presence of God all over those grounds through praise and worship! We release it in prayer using the authority we have to bind and loose, and we stand in the authority of the rhema of God and speak the Word, and the victory is won.

When you go to war and you are challenged by the powers of darkness, how do you react? If you get angry and reactive, the enemy has you. You are out of the Spirit and there is no flow, no worship. There is fear, anger, bitterness, resentment, and hurt. That is why in the midst of the war you need people around you who will be loyal and supportive, who will stand with you so that if you stumble and fumble the ball, they won't stick their cleats in the middle of your back but will lift you up and say, "Let's go at it again."

What happened with David? I am sure that when he killed the lion and the bear, there was a little resistance taking place, but he didn't quit. He learned to prove something. He learned how to pray, to take that slingshot with that little stone and to let it loose and have it strike its mark, so when he went against Goliath he wans't a novice—he knew what was going on.

David couldn't use Saul's armour because it was too big for him. What are you going to wear when you go to battle? Are you going to use my armour? "Well, let's try brother so-and-so." You'd better get your slingshot!

One day the Philistines were going to set Samson up in ambush. They knew he had a supernatural strength that would come on him so they decided to clean the fields of anything he could use for a weapon: rocks, a broken plow, pieces of metal. Oh, there is a jawbone of an ass. That won't do anything. Let's get on; let's go over here. They came upon Samson. He looked around and all he saw was a jawbone of an ass. He picked it up and slew them all.

What does that mean? You know what *your greatest weapon* is besides your worship and your prayer? *That which God has made real to you.* If it hasn't been made alive in your Spirit, it is worthless in warfare. That is what Saul's armour is: someone else's revelation, someone else's experience in God. You might learn from it, but *until it is made alive and built in you, it has no value to you in warfare.* What has been proven in your life? David's slingshot had been proven because he had dealt with the lion and the bear.

Some of our Bible school students have been going through experiences where they haven't had any money and the Lord has provided it. These experiences have caused them to understand what it means to offer up their Isaac. It may not seem as monumental as what happened in Abraham or Moses' life, but that is where they are learning to slay the bear and the lion. It is part of God's preparation, so when they stand against the Goliaths in their life, Goliath will not be someone they weren't prepared to meet; they will already have their proven weapons. Where they have been faithful over a little, God will make them to be rulers over much.

This is true for every one of us; you must allow God to make it a reality for you, and He will do that when the Spirit of God moves on you—which takes us back to worship. We come into His presence with praise and worship. If a church won't worship according to the Word, its life flow will be choked off. God does not say that He is looking for great orators of the Word; He does not say that He is looking for great teachers or evangelists with all nine gifts dripping off their finger tips. But God did say that those who worship Him will worship Him in Spirit and truth and the Father seeks such that will worship Him.

Hear, O my people, and I will testify unto thee O Israel, if Thou wilt hearken unto me. Ps. 81:8

This is God's covenant pledge. Verses 1-7 show man's side of this covenant:

Sing aloud unto God our strength: make a joyful noise unto the God of Jacob. Take a psalm, and bring hither the timbrel, the pleasant harp with the psaltery. Blow up the trumpet in the new moon, in the time appointed, on our solemn feast day. For this was a statute for Israel, and a law of the God of Jacob. This he ordained in Joseph for a testimony, when he went out through the land of Egypt: where I heard a language that I understood not. I removed his shoulder from the burden: his hands were delivered from the pots. Thou calledst in trouble, and I delivered thee; I answered thee in the secret place of thunder: I proved thee at the waters of Meribah.

What is listed here in these conditions of praise? First of all, it says, "Sing unto God." Do you really sing unto the Lord? People who are depressive invariably are not worshipers. There was a wise man who once said, "Let me control the nation's songs and I care not who writes the laws."

Then it says, "Make a joyful noise." "Take a psalm." Sing God's Word! "Bring musical instruments." The trumpet was used to call God's people to assemble for worship and war, and a primary purpose for our coming together is worship. Some want to hold worship as a private thing, but the Scripture makes it congregational. *We come together to worship and commune with God and to glorify His name; not to just hear the Word, not to just have our needs met, but to bless His holy name!* First Peter 2:9 tells us that one of the reasons God has called us is to make us a holy nation, a royal priesthood to show forth the praises of God.

The reason for praise listed in this 81st Psalm: *It was a command to praise the Lord.* If you don't like to praise God, it tells us that your heart isn't where God wants it to be. It also tells us that you are not yet ready for heaven, because when you get up there, there is going to be a lot of worship and if you can't do it now and don't like to be in the presence of worshiping people, you are not going to be happy in heaven! That means you have to let God fit you for heaven.

Next, He said *He ordained praise for a testimony.* The Scripture says in Acts 1:8, "After the Holy Spirit comes upon you, you shall be my witnesses." This means something that you *are*, not something you do, and lifting Jesus up in worship is one of the ways that we *are* witnesses.

Then He says, "I remove his shoulder from the burden." One of the things that happens *as we worship is the burdens are lifted.* Another thing that begins to happen is *God answers prayer* and we begin to pass tests that we previously failed.

In verses 9 and 10, He says if we worship like that:

There shall no strange god be in thee; neither shalt thou worship any strange god. I am the Lord thy God, which brought thee out of the land of Egypt: open thy mouth wide, and I will fill it.

The context of the phrase "open thy mouth wide and I will fill it" is to fill it with praise and worship.

Then He talks about how Israel would not do it:

But my people would not hearken to my voice; and Israel would none of me. So I gave them up unto their own hearts' lust: and they walked in their own counsels.

Oh that my people had hearkened unto me, and Israel had walked in my ways! I should soon have subdued their enemies, and turned my hand against their adversaries. The haters of the Lord should have submitted themselves unto him: but their time should have endured forever. He should have fed them also with the finest of the wheat; and with the honey out of the rock should I have satisfied thee. V. 13-16

When we keep the covenant of worship, we learn that God says He will subdue our enemies, and turn His hand against our adversaries. Those that hate the Lord will submit themselves unto Him. We continue to endure, are not put down and He will establish us. Would we be fed with the leftovers of the wheat? No, the finest of the wheat and with the honey out of the rock. Another place where we see honey in the Scripture is when Jonathan had taken that great victory, set forth his sword, took the honey that dripped from the trees, tasted it, and his eyes were enlightened: the revelation of God unfolding. That would have been rich and satisfying to Israel.

We have with this concept of praying in the Spirit the thought of not being in the flesh, having the mind of Christ, the will of God; we have a concept of praying in tongues until we come into a place where we can articulate the mind of Christ in intercession. We understand that an intercessor is one who takes the place of another. We learn that as we worship, God intervenes on our behalf and we find that He gives us His will, speaks to us, and our enemies are overthrown. We learn that as we come to God in war, these things must be made a reality to us—we cannot wear someone else's armour. When you get into the battle and try to worship, it is going to be empty if you are not a worshiper all the time; you will be looking through Saul's armour. When you get to the battle, you will not discern God's voice if you have not learned to hear from Him in the regular walk of your life. To be a worshiper is not something that you do on Sunday morning and Sunday night and Wednesday. *It is a daily lifestyle.*

Father, as we have come to the conclusion of our study, there is so much that we have learned about warfare. Lord, as we come into this realm of prayer in the Spirit and intercession and worship, there is so little that can really be taught by words. We learn to worship by worshiping and we learn to pray by praying. We learn to be an intercessor by opening our spirits to your Spirit and allowing You to flow through us. We learn to enter into your presence and commune with You in worship as our hearts are drawn towards You to bless You. Father, we can't go to war and be effective without being worshipers, without learning to offer continually the sacrifice of praise which is the fruit of our lips. Father, there will be times in the midst of the battle where everything we feel will be not to worship; we won't feel like it. We might be facing fear, we might be facing grief, we might be facing a grievous failure. We might be facing all kinds of things, Lord, but what our circumstances are do not change the fact that You are worthy to be worshiped and we must come to a place where we have cultivated worship independent of our circumstances, to worship You and to bless You. As the Psalmist David said, "Soul, why are you downcast within me? Bless the Lord, oh my soul and all that is within me, bless His holy name." We learn to worship as a matter of war and to worship as a matter of blessing You. We learn to worship as a matter of Christian survival. And through worship comes intercession. As we draw near to You, Lord, we will begin to feel your heartbeat and begin to sense your cry for a lost and dying world. Lord, we can't get close to You without sensing the heart that would send His Son to die in our place. We can't come close to You without seeking the cry of your Spirit for those who have not yet heard, and that is where burden and travail and intercession come as we get close to the heart of God. Draw us to yourself and teach us to be effective channels of your life in this needy world. Amen.

Roger Houtsma World Outreach

In addition to his Pastoral ministry, Dr. Houtsma ministers in Crusades throughout the world as a Missionary Evangelist. Crowds of up to 150,000 have attended a single service in which they have witnessed outstanding miracles of healing of every manner of disease and infirmity. Along with the Crusades, Dr. Houtsma holds a special Minister's Institute to instruct the National Ministers in the methods and principles of ministry with God's miracle power that have been so effective in his meetings. Many National Ministers have testified to being broken through into a true ministry with God's supernatural power as a result of these meetings. Over 30,000 ministers have been trained to date.

For information write:
Roger Houtsma
World Outreach
P.O. Box 950
Novato, CA 94948 USA